Wild Things

Poems of Grief and Love, Loss and Gratitude

Roberta C. Bondi

UPPER
ROOM BOOKS®
NASHVILLE

WILD THINGS

POEMS OF GRIEF AND LOVE, LOSS AND GRATITUDE

© 2014 by Roberta Bondi. All rights reserved.

UPPER ROOM', UPPER ROOM BOOKS' and design logos are trademarks owned by THE UPPER ROOM', a ministry of GBOD,' Nashville, Tennessee. All rights reserved.

The Upper Room Books website: books.upperroom.org

Cover design: Kara Davison/Faceout Studio, faceoutstudio.com

Cover image: © Paul Grand / Trevillion Images

LIBRARY OF CONGRESS CATALOGING-IN-PUBLICATION DATA

Bondi, Roberta C.
[Short stories. Selections]
Wild things : poems of grief and love, loss and gratitude / Roberta C. Bondi.
    pages cm
Includes index.
ISBN 978-0-8358-1363-1 (print)—ISBN 978-0-8358-1364-8 (mobi) — ISBN 978-0-8358-1365-5 (epub)
I. Title.
PS3602.O65666W55 2014
811'.6—dc23
                                                        2013051124

Printed in the United States of America

Contents

Chapter 1 The Experience of Her Death 21

Chapter 2 Easter and Thereabouts 37

Chapter 3 Family, Friends, and the Communion of the Saints 49

Chapter 4 Time and Memory 65

Chapter 5 Household Goods 81

Chapter 6 *Loss* *87*

Chapter 7 *Healing Begins* *101*

Chapter 8 *Weaving* *119*

Chapter 9 Wild Things 137

Chapter 10 The Great Mystery 155

Why These Poems Matter

*H*ow does a person tolerate the intolerable, bear the unbearable?

I have known Roberta Bondi since 1979 when she joined the faculty of Candler School of Theology at Emory University. I was a colloquy leader in the first class she taught and a student in her first seminar. I was also a student in the first class her husband, Richard, taught. Later, when Richard switched careers, I served as the director of his pastoral counselor training program. For the past ten years, Richard and I have been colleagues at the Emmanuel Center for Pastoral Counseling. Richard and Roberta are now my dear friends.

As Roberta watched her mother age, she would wonder aloud, "How will I continue my life when my mother is not in it? I cannot imagine that world."

So, as Mrs. Cowan's death approached, those of us who loved Roberta felt concerned about how she would cope. I was relieved when Roberta's poems started arriving in my inbox. The poems gave voice to her grief. In voicing her grief, she moved through it rather than being lost in it. In that process she also created a resource for others.

A person's grieving distorts time; color disappears. Life around the grieving person continues in a way that he or she finds disorienting. Emotions come and go in ways that make no sense to the grief-stricken, much less to others. The one grieving may wonder if she or he is going crazy now, losing all of life—not just the person who is no longer in it. In times such as these, it helps to know that you are not crazy; you are grieving. This is what the experience of grief looks like and feels like.

Few books articulate grief in a way that people can identify with it while they grieve. But when someone articulates your pain—particularly someone you trust who offers more than simple platitudes, someone who felt what you are feeling and made it through—you find comfort. You think, *If she can survive, I can survive also. And perhaps, eventually, even be glad to have done so.*

Through these poems, Roberta has created this kind of resource. Grief involves the whole person, and her acknowledgment of this fact enriches her writing. Roberta, aware of and able to articulate her feelings, is an artist, attentive to detail. She shares a deep connection to nature and in the cycles of creation finds hope for recovery. But most of all, she is a lover of God. Through her years of study, teaching, and prayer she has come to know in her bones that she, like all of us, is God's Beloved. These qualities come to bear on her experience, available to those who ponder her words.

People tell me that they do not want to stop grieving because grief is their last connection to their loved one. When it goes away, they fear the person will really be gone. I understand that. The alternative is to find the person's presence in a new way in their lives: in memories, objects, experiences, and understanding. As Roberta describes her encounters with nature, her gradual re-engagement of her work as a weaver, her memories of her mother and their mutual relatives, she provides an example of how to know the loved one's presence in new ways.

The prologue of John's Gospel closes with these words: "The light shines in the darkness and the darkness did not overcome it." It does not say the light overcame the dark, only that the dark did not overcome the light. Grief can be a dark place. People can fear going into that dark. But if they have light it provides hope that they will not become lost in the dark.

These poems are an embodiment of grief and pain but also of love and hope, of God's relentless and enduring love. They are a source of light for others who find themselves in the dark. I look forward to being able to give this book to clients so that Roberta can be their companion as they make their way through the darkness of grief, so that her words can remind them that through it all they are held and sustained by God and the human family.

—TERE TYNER CANZONERI, MDiv, LCSW
Diplomate American Association of Pastoral Counselors

Acknowledgments

So many people helped me in the months after my mother's last week of life, and all of them have contributed directly or indirectly to this book. The two most important, however, are my husband, Richard Bondi, and my friend and long-ago former student, Sharon Watkins. Sharon was there with her physical presence, her phone calls, her daily support, and her willingness to read the poems as I wrote them. When Mama died, Sharon and her husband, Jerry, along with a dear former student Ike Parker and his partner, Dick, drove a long way from North Georgia to come to the memorial service in Louisville, Kentucky. Their presence filled my heart with gratitude and a little easing of the pain. As for Richard, he encouraged me from the beginning to keep in mind the possibility of collecting the poems at some point to make them available to people who might share in them and benefit from them. Furthermore, every day those first months, I would send the poems to Richard as I wrote them, and every day he would read them and respond to them with focus, appreciation, support, and love. Without his encouragement, perhaps there would have been no poems, for it had been a long time since I had written anything. Now, at the end of the project, he has put his considerable editing and computer skills to use in order to present a usable manuscript to the press. I don't believe I could have done this in less than a year or two, if at all. However much I thank him, it is not enough.

Only a few people besides Richard read all the poems every day: CeCe Balboni, Sharon Watkins, Myra Kibler, my former student and dear friend Tere Canzoneri, and Cindy Avens and Dick Zeller. Lewis Ayres also read all of the poems but in clumps. Of these friends, Sharon Watkins, Myra Kibler, Tere Canzoneri, and Cindy Avens read through the lot of them at the end and made suggestions on how to arrange them. This helped me greatly.

Many friends read some of the poems and gave me feedback at one point or another. Among them are Steve Martin, Patti Park, Jo Kingsman, Patout Burns (whose background and training in spiritual direction served me well when I most needed it), Pat Luna, Karen Scheib, Steve Stevens, and Millie Hastings.

Then, there is my family, whom I want to thank for their unflagging support. I am very grateful to my daughter, Anna Trodglen, and my son, Ben Chesnut. I also thank my dear brothers, Fred and Wesley Cowan, and my sisters-in-law, Linda and Shelley, all of whom exhibited saving levels of kindness, gentleness, and intelligence throughout those first terrible days.

Finally, I want to thank Curly, my little white dog, whom I got out of bed and walked every day. Curly is a slow and inquisitive walker, so he gave me the opportunity to really see and live in the natural world around me. He also made himself available for cuddling when I most needed it. How does anybody finally begin to heal without an animal?

Introduction for My Readers

*M*ama's death shocked me. It shocked my whole being, body and soul, to lose my mother. It wasn't a surprise; she was two days short of her ninety-sixth birthday, after all, but it was impossible to prepare myself in advance. I acknowledged the peculiarly inescapable quality of mother-daughter relationships as my grandmothers and great-grandmothers, aunts and great-aunts, as well as my mother, always described it. Now I had found it out for myself: when mother died, there was too much to feel; there were too many losses to grieve, to remember, to think about, to pray over; and also too many contradictory experiences and emotions to carry at once without bursting open.

Twenty years ago, my primary means of surviving Mama's death and living in it would have come through writing about it. The last book I had written caused great pain inadvertently to a lot of people I loved, and I had utterly lost my taste for writing. I walked away from it. In losing my writing, however, I seemed to have lost a vital part of myself, and I grieved this loss deeply.

Then Mama died, and I suddenly discovered that my words had been given back to me. I began to write again. Where the well had been dry, now poems rose up in me and overflowed. With the new words came an easing of pain (some days more than others), gratitude for my mother's gifts and our seventy-one years together, a sense of the great mystery of life and death, of loss, of the goodness of God, of the erasing of time in our human love for each other. With these words, spoken in my heart before they were ever written down, came long-forgotten memories of times that sucked me back into them as though they were taking place in the present. And then I experienced a heightened awareness in my ability to see—*really* see—what was around me and also to smell and taste and sense touch.

All these sensations, I know now, characterize not just my own grief but common grief in the face of loss. Grief sears our hearts but can also bring great gifts. The fact that we would gladly exchange those gifts for the lives of our beloved dead does not make them less real. They are precious, perhaps to be received in no other way. We may reject them or accept them with a gratitude that comes as the greatest gift of all, for gratitude is not an attitude we can produce simply by gritting our teeth.

When we grieve, we seldom grieve alone. I was not thinking about this fact at all the week before Mama died. In fact, my pain seemed to be my own, mine and that of my brothers and sisters, children, and nieces and nephews. By the time of Mama's funeral and memorial service, I had come to my senses and could pay attention. Very soon I knew in every cell of my body that we all suffer grief, but in this time of suffering we find ourselves solidly sustained by one another, by those we know and those we will never know, by all who live and have ever lived, whom we love and who love us without our even realizing it.

Not surprisingly, I wasn't thinking of you, my readers, when I first began my poems. It never occurred to me that as we sustain one another in our grieving, my writing that proved so useful to me would be useful to others as well. Furthermore, if other people could find my words useful for understanding or comforting or giving words to their grief, it would be a gift for both of us. I sincerely hope this happens for you. While this book has been written from the perspective of one who grieves, I am hoping that others can also benefit from it. I'm thinking of those who might one day grieve, which I assure you will be all of us in this world. I'm also thinking of those who seek to aid and comfort those who do grieve now: pastoral counselors and other therapists; hospice workers; chaplains, spiritual directors; ministers and seminarians; and the family and friends of those undergoing loss.

I can't presume to tell you what do do with these poems—they are a gift, after all—but I have a few suggestions for how you might use them, which I will get to in a moment. First, I would like to tell you a little about my Mama, whose loss has brought all this about, and my relationship with her.

About Mama

Mama was born in 1917 on a small farm in Union County in western Kentucky, in the family house we always heard called "the House on the Hill." She was the oldest child of seven children, a girl born into a very large extended family that was a matriarchy. Her own mother, whom my family members called Panny, was the oldest child as well as the oldest girl in her generation. This large farming family was close, hard-working (there is no other way to live on a farm), cheerful, competitive, full of humor. There were also lawyers sprinkled around, as there still are, and an occasional doctor, but basically life entailed life on the farm.

To my knowledge, mother was the first one of us (and the last of her generation) to go off to take up life in the big city. I am not sure how Mama felt about it at first, but Panny was determined that her first daughter would "make something of herself" in the wide world. Panny sent Mama to commercial school in Louisville to learn to be a secretary. After graduation she went farther away still, taking a job in Cincinnati, Ohio. Not long after that, she met my father, an exotic young man who had grown up in Manhattan.

Mama was crazy about him, and within two months they had married. Two years later I was born, then my brother Fred after four more years, and Wesley ten years later.

Within the next few years my mother and father lived in Birmingham, Alabama; the borough of Queens in New York; and finally Wilmington, Delaware. Tragically, after fourteen years of marriage, these two proud people who truly loved each other divorced. Mama never got over it.

And Mama was, indeed, proud. As a woman who had spent all her married years as a housewife, she suddenly found herself with enormous grief, little money, rusty skills, and three children to support—children for whom she had high hopes. The early 1950s was a bad time to find herself in this position.

But mother was indomitable, as she was all her life. After a brief return to her parents' farm, she settled us in Louisville, Kentucky, enrolled us in school, and with the help of my Great-Aunt Nacky (who was great in about every way you could name) returned to secretarial school for a refresher course and then got herself a job. Later, while I was in college, again with Aunt Nacky's help, Mama got a college degree herself. Amazingly, she supported us all on her salary through the years, along with some child support money. There was no extra money, but we had what we needed, including mother's constant expectation that we three would go to college and eventually "make something of ourselves." How she did it, I don't know. But by the time we did go to college, with the help of scholarships, she had saved what we needed for school. All three of us ended up with advanced degrees, which, while we were in school and not earning incomes, I am fairly sure she often felt was a bit much, even for her ambitious dreams for us.

As is true in so many mother-daughter relations, my relationship with Mama was not always easy: tight bonds can make for irritability or worse, as well as situations in which it is hard for the daughter to tell where mother ends and she begins, and vice versa. How many times I heard her say, and never positively, "When you act like that, it reflects on me!"

In the 1950s people highly valued "being normal," and, for one reason or another, I didn't make the cut. Mama expected me to grow up and be a housewife, cooking well, ironing the sheets, keeping the baseboards clean, raising babies, obeying my husband—just as she had intended for herself. That is what women were supposed to do with their lives. There was no women's movement yet, at least none available to me, but I knew I couldn't live this life that had nearly broken my mother when she was divorced. I believe she wanted more for me, but at the same time, she wanted me to be a woman with the gifts and skills of my high-achieving, farm-women relatives.

This role disagreement affected both of us in my early years, bringing frustration and disappointment. I couldn't be who she wanted me to be or at least who I thought she wanted me to be. In spite of her doubts about the life I had chosen and continued to choose, she supported me. Whatever she thought about the values she espoused with one part of herself, she was, at the same time, a fierce feminist before her time who wanted me to be independent and support myself and my children more easily than she. She felt sure my husband would leave me like hers had.

So, Mama came and cared for the children at several critical times while I wrote my dissertation. The children adored her. She would come and cook and mind them and the house and leave me feeling loved and taken care of. She sewed a wardrobe for me so that I could look professional. (I still don't know how to sew.) She bought my first electric typewriter and then my first computer and my first dishwasher.

She also would regularly tell me to hold my shoulders up because I looked awful if I didn't (I'm a lifelong, dedicated sloucher) and that I needed to lose weight. Or she would congratulate me when I had lost weight "because you look so much cuter thin." She always made critical remarks about professors who thought they were so smart just because they were academics, and she loved jokes of which they were the butt. Once in her old age I told her it hurt me when she found fault with me. She was shocked when I said it, then she laughed. "Honey, I just do it because I love you. I just want you to be perfect," she said, half meaning it and half not.

In her later years, Mama had fully converted to feminism and the rights of women, including equal pay for equal work, which paralleled her distrust of men. If I worried about the house, she would say, "Oh, who cares. You have too much to do to think about that." In my last working years I had her unrelenting support.

When I was young, I felt proud of Mama—in a grudging sort of way—for the many things she could do that I couldn't. Now I am incredibly proud of her for who she was. She became a teacher for children with reading disabilities when she got through college, and she loved those children to the day she died. "I miss the little children," she said wistfully when she was in her nineties. She was creative, a quilt maker and an artist of a cook. She taught us children to value beauty. She read good books and kept up with current events until she lost her eyesight. An ardent lover of our huge extended family, she kept track of everybody and attended to marriages, births, deaths, and graduations. In her last years at the retirement home, she got to know all those who worked there and befriended them, and they returned that friendship. Her life had been hard, but it was a good one. In spite of the loss of my father, she felt truly blest to love and be loved as she was.

It was important for her to be a good person, and she worked at it her whole life. This meant being generous and looking after others who needed it. Even at age ninety-one or ninety-two, she was still visiting the "old women" in her retirement home who were shut-ins, although most were much younger than she was. She ended every phone conversation we ever had by saying, "Save your money!" or "Now be a good girl!" I tried to do both.

She was the most powerful person in my life until she reached her nineties and started to decline. Then, in her last years, our roles reversed, as is true in so many parent-child relationships. Though I lived far away, she came to lean on me and need my love and support in new ways with the innocent trust of a loved child. We daughters always need our mothers, and I still needed her right until the end when she became feeble and deaf. I wanted to protect her from suffering, but I couldn't do it. Old age brings many gifts, but it also brings real pain that not even our loving God will shield us from because it inevitably goes with our mortality.

Mama's death left me with a horrendous number of conflicting feelings in my grief—love, pain, anger, guilt, emptiness, too much fullness, confusion, exhaustion, relief that she was no longer suffering. And along with all these emotions I experienced, and still do, an overwhelming sense of the kindness, goodness, and trustworthiness of God's steady presence, a sense so strong that I can say that the experience of my mother's death was equally an experience of God. For all of this, I am filled with gratitude and love as well as a pain I suspect will not be gone for a long time.

Reading the Book

This is a book of poetry, not a manual. It is my gift to you of my own experiences and thoughts. I cannot tell you how to use it, but I will suggest how it can help in a time of grief.

First, I have sorted the poems by topics arranged in chapters. You do not have to read one poem after another. Read where your fancy takes you. If you would find it useful to read the poems in chronological order, I provide an index of their titles arranged by date. (See page 171.)

Grief is such a messy thing. It fills us with many ideas and images, memories and fantasies, celebration and bitter regret all at once—all superimposed upon one another. No wonder it wears us out. I hope you read this book and find help to recognize and aid you in sorting out your own conflicting feelings. May the poems give rise to your own words if you need them.

Many of these poems describe my own memories and my mulling over the meanings in them. May they inspire you to remember your life as it becomes present to you in the loss you are living through. May they give you a hand as you try to make sense of all that's happening and accept it with gratitude and love.

I would also hope the poems to be a tool for your recognizing how tied together we all are, for seeing that none of us is a separate individual who formed herself or himself all alone—and for recognizing the goodness and wonder of these connections. That goodness and wonder can surface particularly in our closest relationships: between mothers and grown children, parents and children still in our immediate care. As I mentioned, that closeness makes it hard to tell where one of us leaves off and another begins.

On the other hand, I have received great comfort from knowing that humans suffer the experience of loss by virtue of being human. All of us are subject to it, and so no one can truthfully say, "There is no one else in the universe who knows what I feel." However isolated we may feel in other areas of our lives, in our grief we are not isolated at all; we have with us not only the presence of God but the whole human race solidly with us, supporting us even when we do not allow ourselves to feel it.

The event of death is not separate from all other life events. My mother's death has been and continues to be a lens through which I can see the many layers of meaning in my life. May this book aid you in recognizing how your loss can also provide a lens for you.

Finally, may these poems help you in further opening your senses in all their acuteness to see the wondrous beauty and goodness of the natural world around you, to take in sights and sounds and smells. May they offer comfort as you move increasingly into gratitude for life, gratitude for what we all have been given, and most of all, for the reality and presence of God who makes all things, sustains all things, and most surely heals all things.

May your heart be comforted, my friend.

The Experience of Her Death

*T*he phone call I had been dreading for so long came to me a week before Mama died. My brother Fred, distraught, said to me, "It's Mama. She can't talk!" I had customarily called Mama on the phone every night for some time. I realized she was having difficulty speaking, but it didn't seem as bad as he made it sound. "Let me talk with her," I answered, expecting, indeed, that it wouldn't be so bad. The only trouble was, it was that bad.

"I can't talk," Mama struggled to articulate. She wanted to know why she couldn't speak. She was desperate.

I could understand all this clearly enough, and I continued to be able to make sense of what Mama said for the next week, though I don't know how. After dithering a little while, I made a plane reservation and flew to Louisville the next day, a week before Palm Sunday.

As for why I dithered, I can only say this: I wasn't prepared. We can never really be prepared for a parent's death or a child's death or the death of anyone we love. I wanted my brother to be exaggerating—*needed* my brother to be exaggerating—but as I learned soon enough, he wasn't.

It reminds me now of the call I received on Good Friday morning telling me that my very sick father had died—the year I turned fifty. "Are you sure?" I asked stupidly, the tears running down my face in torrents. "Are you really sure?" All the while I wondered if the world could go on as usual if he weren't in it. Now it was the same for Mama, only more so.

Our mothers, after all, were the the only ones whose wombs we grew in, who delivered us into a world at first almost entirely governed by them, whose faces we first learned, and who made it increasingly clear to us that we had faces too. We learned love from our mothers and how to ask for what we needed. If we were lucky our mothers provided for us. Our mothers were the mattresses in our cribs, the air we breathed, the lens through which we saw the world. (Nowadays, fathers often do all these things as well. But when I was a baby, mothers were the primary caregivers.)

We never forget these qualities of our early lives. In our hearts, even if we are angry with our mothers or disappointed or feel betrayed by them or have been badly hurt by them or don't even want them (and some people really have had experiences that make them feel this way), none of us can simply shuck our mothers off. Our deepest physical and emotional bonds remain with our mothers in spite of ourselves. This seems especially true with women.

At any rate, over the next week, Mama's impending death grew more terrible than I could have imagined. She was very frightened and couldn't get her breath, and I couldn't comfort her. At the same time, however, my two brothers and sisters-in-law (sisters, really), and all her beloved grandchildren except one were with her. For me, being with my family brought a deep comfort so grounded in God's love that I will always wonder at it and be grateful for it.

Why do we suffer in pain and fear as human beings? I could have asked that question during this time of Mama's passing, but I didn't. I knew that God loves us and is with us. Through the entire experience of Mama's dying, I never raised that question. All Mama's suffering took place in God, in God's love, and I never doubted it. More primitive feelings arose in me: feelings of loss, guilt, and pain—sometimes anger. God held all my feelings, but that didn't keep the feelings from being painfully real.

I survived the pain by writing daily as the experience unfolded. These are my poems, but they are also a journal. If you are grieving, may they offer you a way to live through your pain.

Writing as My Mother Dies

I can't imagine how I ever thought it is writing that hurts.
Living is what does it.
Writing shapes the pain that is already there into something else,
though what that something else is, I could hardly say.

My mother's eyes
in which I was conceived,
carried, and finally born—
only words release me into separate life and even then it is not all
    that separate.

The Word made flesh
is also made once again only word,
but spoken and spoken again

whispered, shouted, mumbled,
sighed and sung until I vibrate like a glass under a wet finger.

My mother spoken into life
is now being spoken out of it
to some place where she always has been, anyway.
To some place I may be even now.
Perhaps where Eve (with the help of Adam)
at the foot of Jacob's ladder
named the animals,
and smiled,
and counted angels.

Mama Who Is Dying

Mama, your voice is in my ears as though you are a young woman,
not ninety-six and old and mostly beside yourself with pain and
   exhaustion and a mind that
isn't quite here or not here.

Your moans, which are very real, are not so loud in my mind
as your laughter as you talk to your sisters.

Your eyes are brown and beautiful,
your mouth drawn together almost into a whistle.

It is strange that it is not your former hurt or anger or disappointment
   with your life
since Daddy left you that makes the air around you vibrate.

It is your joy and energy, your power of love that are present now
   as your body dies.

Why have I not seen it before but only known your sorrow?

How can this happen now? Is time not real at all?

Are you truly stepping out of that old stuff
as you might
leave a pair of dirty jeans right inside the door?

Is my real Mama here?

Mama, wherever you are going, wherever you have gone,
don't forget me.

I Think I May Be Grieving

I think I may be grieving.
Where else can my calm have come from?
Not from the hills, that's for sure.

I sit on Mama's couch,
and I can't imagine this house
razed and plowed under like her mother's was.

There is nothing here that Mama didn't love.
All of it beautiful because it was beautiful to her.

Every one of us,
daughters, sons,
each beloved grandchild,
daughters and sons-in-law,
her own mama and daddy,
her dear sisters and brothers,
ancient aunts and great-aunts
as far back as you can go.
Her parents' grandparents,
babies, cousins,
nieces and nephews,
all in pictures, a whole company of what, exactly?

Paperweights, the dishes she bought
when we moved to Louisville
(she was so proud of them—
now they are stained and chipped),
my grandmother's clock
she longed for in her own last years.

Embroidered linens, a few remaining quilts
she hasn't given away.
And then, the solid furniture,
chairs, tables, chests,

and the not so solid—
sofa, rug, mirrors,
many mirrors, beautiful carved frames.
So many faces in them all at once,
cloudy but there.

Lamps. Bowls.
Towels, combs, lotions,
paper bags (hard to find nowadays)
plastic bags, toilet paper,
cloth bags,
old clothes (there are no favorites now;
even the good ones look crumpled and ugly).

Oh, Mama, I know you are held safe in God.
But I can't breathe and my chest hurts.
Everything about this hurts.

Everything about This Hurts

Worst of all is when they turn you in the bed.
Your breathing
is labored, as they say.
My own lungs choke for you.

You don't sigh anymore
under the smoothing of morphine,
but we can see that you are afraid.

"How much longer?"
you ask in those
few times you might be conscious.

Soon, Mama, soon, we say,
and we hope it will be true.

Gentle, Gentle

Gentle, gentle.
They love their grandmother so much,
these grown, good grandchildren.
They are as gentle with her as—
well, there are no words for it,
only gentle.
Gentle

Holy Spirit, supply the breath,
carry the life,
quench the burning in my mother's throat,
ease the hurt.
Gentle, gentle
mercy, mercy.

The Eighth Day

Fog this morning,
sun burning it off now,
shining drops of water
hanging from every hemlock needle,
daytime stars.

I slept well last night
except I woke up sore
every two or three hours,
having lain in one spot for hours.

Mother cried out when they would turn her in her bed,
terrible cries of terror and maybe pain.
It made me never want to sleep again.
I wanted to keep watch with her,
to watch over her.
My body finally said, "Enough"
but my eyes never left her face.

Two Days Till Your Birthday

Two days till your birthday.
Earlier this week you kept asking
"Is it my birthday yet?"
Then you would ask,
"When will this be over?"

Now you ask nothing,
and I ask nothing too.
The paper is too hard for me.
The AARP magazine is beyond me,
though it ought to be just right.
But it isn't. It's for the living,
and I am way beyond that.

When I was younger,
in my thirties, say,
or my fifties,
I didn't know where mother ended
and I began.

It's not like that now,
at least not exactly.
I am hemmed in before and behind,
and I imagine I am content with this.

I stare at the floor,
my heartbeat slow,
my breathing even slower.

God is here,
love is strong.
I believe in resurrection.
It's just that now it is so irrelevant.

Two or Three Days After I Arrived

Two or three days after I arrived in Louisville,
you were lying in bed, hurting,
not looking at me,
and I had my face down close to yours,
looking at you and hurting.

All at once, like a flash of blinding sun,
you opened your eyes and smiled at me,
your first smile since I got there
(you had been straining to breathe,
gasping and choking).
It was a startling smile, familiar and beloved.

"Look at your hair!" you cried in your old way,
clear enough,
though where your voice came from,
I can't possibly know.
Your face lit up like nobody else's could,
with pleasure and with something else.

The fact is, it was with mischief.
"Let me feel it!" you said, as though
you were sure you oughtn't,
sure you were going to get away with something.

A miracle, your old voice,
full of a kind of delightful greediness
and fun I hadn't heard for such a long time.

I put my face closer.
Slowly you lifted your hand
and patted my hair.

"It is so soft!" you said.
Your voice was full of wonder.
Then, still smiling, you closed your eyes and slept.

You know, I'd never had curly hair until last summer
(it began to curl then by itself after I missed
a haircut or two)
and you just couldn't get over it.
"Look at those curls," you said, again and again.
"I just hate you!"

I knew this wasn't what you meant.
I believe you took my hair as my highest accomplishment
and yours too, since you were my mother.
Everything I did reflected on you.

I ponder it and ponder it.
each curly hair,
the whole business, start to finish,
a gift, a joy, a resurrection.

News

I'm reading the news this morning;
haven't done that in a while.
Bird flu in China,
mining disaster in Tibet,
no new immigration from Mexico—
What a relief!
I ought to be ashamed.

Not Quite Liminal

We have all been visiting
the great open space
into which mother was just born.
We have followed her as far as we could.
"Good-bye, good-bye,"
we call.
"Soon enough
we will be born ourselves
into where you are.
Hold a place for us."

In all this,
our ordinary has been displaced
by mystery,
by a beauty that is felt in the bone,
not seen, not heard.

But the everyday is coming back now,
seeping in from the bottom
through some soft hidden spring.

The blessed ordinary.
Now I look below me and see:
The dark red buds of maple trees,
the white of late Bradford pears,
daffodils fading,
forsythia celebrating,
the greenest grass imaginable that only
comes at Easter.

I see the river, brown from the rain;
titmice at the hole in the white oak tree,
goldfinches turning gold again
after their drab winter.

I see the children, some happy, some not;
friends together, walking;
strangers whose secret hearts are
turned with love toward other strangers.

I see everything in this ordinary world,
precious and rare,
lovable beyond anything.
I long to love it all
until I die.

Easter and Thereabouts

*W*hen it came time to marry, Easter weekend seemed exactly right to Richard and me. It wasn't liturgically correct according to church tradition, but it was decidedly right in our interior liturgical calendars. Our decision to marry then had been sudden: We decided over the phone on Palm Sunday, invited family and friends, and celebrated the next Sunday. Mama came down from Louisville with her best friend by Thursday, and the two of them cooked and cleaned (as much as was possible with an incontinent, demented cat whose favorite spot was the dining room rug), and finally, decorated the house with flowers from the yard. Richard arrived Friday from Milwaukee, where he had been teaching, and we went immediately for blood tests and paperwork.

It was a hectic but wonderfully happy season. The dogwoods and azaleas were blooming as only they can in Atlanta during the spring. There were tiny bright green leaves on the trees and bushes and a lot of long silky new grass. I remember in an almost hallucinatory way walking outside with Richard after the ceremony and finding myself in that sweet-smelling space. Probably, rabbits congregated in the bushes around the dogwood tree. Though we never saw them, I could feel them there, and that seemed appropriate. All in all, a wonderful day—the day we came rejoicing, forgetting our sorrows, and bringing in the sheaves.

Easter has not always been a happy time since for me, however. Twenty-two years ago on Holy Thursday, long after Richard and I were married, I received a call from my brother Fred. My father had died after a year of hiding his illness from his own children. My relationship with him, while painful and difficult most of my life, carried much love.

Richard arranged for us to fly to Connecticut the next day. It was raining so hard in Georgia that the plane could not take off for many hours after we got to the airport. Finally, upon landing, I recall being met by a gracious limo driver and his friend who drove us from LaGuardia to the funeral home where Daddy was. And very clearly, I remember sobbing as I saw him lying in the casket, looking exactly like himself down to the buttons on his blazer.

Tears were the main thing. I had begun to cry the moment that first call came telling me of his death, and I could not stop crying right up until his funeral. I never slept; I cried and called out his name throughout the night. I am crying now as I remember it; I don't think grief ever goes entirely away.

One church tradition celebrates Holy Saturday, Jesus' day in the tomb, as the day Jesus rescues all the dead from the time of Adam and Eve onward. A text from the ancient church describes the event in this way: Jesus leaps from the cross into that place of death, takes hold of the hands of Eve and Adam who hold hands with the other dead around them, and grasping them all firmly and securely, leaps out again. It is fanciful, I know. But at my father's funeral on that Holy Saturday so many centuries later, it meant everything to me. It began with the priest addressing my father in his casket reminding him how, when he had been baptized, he had been baptized into the death and resurrection of Christ. Now what had once taken place in symbol was happening in reality in the waters of his physical death.

The priest's words came as gift. At the very moment I heard them, I was filled with certainty that my father on that Holy Saturday had been met in death by Jesus Christ, God's own self. He was not alone but safe in God. It was then that I stopped crying. The whole of Easter, the whole three days of it, right through to the Resurrection, had become more real than anything else on earth.

This was not my experience when Mama died. She died the same week as Daddy—only twenty-two years later. She also died in the days before Easter—her death caught up in this sacred time. Her passing occurred on Palm Sunday, and we buried her on Wednesday of that week in Union County, Kentucky, alongside her parents. Her memorial service in Louisville was the next day, Holy Thursday, the day Daddy had died.

But what different experiences these two deaths were! With Daddy, I lived intensely through the whole Easter season. With Mama, I don't remember arriving at Easter itself. For me, it was Good Friday all the way, grieving and grieving. Not that there was nothing to celebrate that Sunday: We celebrated her life and the love that surrounded her and us. We acknowledged the kindness of those who cared for her and for us in that awful time and the gift of gratitude we felt for her love and for each other. We rejoiced in God's love and the goodness and beauty of life itself. But that day of resurrection left me with more grief than joy.

I believe the experiences of our loved ones' deaths differ from one another, depending on our relationship with the person and where we are in our life at the time. No roadmap shows how to get through, and none will ever exist. Our feelings will always be legion and inconsistent—conflicting feelings residing together with no difficulty at all. Very little about grief is easy; very little is not messy, exhausting, confusing.

As for myself, when I think back over these two deaths, I am only certain of one thing: I will never again live through Easter in the same way. It will always be the time of my marriage, but just as much it is the time of Daddy's and Mama's deaths. Though this is painful, it somehow feels right.

Clothes

They tell us to bring an outfit for Mama to wear.
But the casket will be closed! we cry.
You never know, says the funeral director, with his sad smile,
someone might want to see her.

Not me, I think. O God, not me.

Something comfortable, I say,
a sweater I made her once
from soft lamb's wool I dyed and spun myself.
And one of her dollies too,
so she will have someone to take care of.

Soft slippers, nothing tight
to wear to sleep in your last house.

March 26, Your Birthday

You died two days ago, Palm Sunday.
Today it's snowing,
cold, white and black branches,
white earth, clothing for a bride,
but cold. The sky clothes everything.

You made your own wedding dress,
before you knew what it would be.
We have it, now, dark brown rayon
with a tiny, random pattern of white.
There are three little green glass buttons.
Perfectly round, perfectly not matching what you
had made.

That dress is so small!

(We would have buried you in it, but it would never fit.
You are so much larger than it was.
As large as a mountain or the white sky.)

I imagine Daddy thought it beautiful,
because you were beautiful.
It matched
those eyes you had and never lost,
the same ones you opened to look
at me in your last moment
when I told you I loved you
and held your hand.

Oh Mama, Mama.
What still makes your eyes so deep and shiny?
Were your tears always there
even though you were the first and favorite child
of Panny and Papa Charles

and all those doting aunts and uncles
back to antiquity?

It was Palm Sunday, with tears accompanying the palms
and shouting crowds.
You can't die! They cried out.
You are the ground under our feet,
the air we breathe!
You are our king!
But Jesus knew what was coming.

We knew what was coming,
and we cried out too.

For Her Memorial:
They Were All Easter Clothes

Mama sewed as far back as I can remember.
What she made between the time she married
and when I was born, I can't imagine.

I must have been a year or so old
when she sewed us matching dresses—
white with tiny lilacs and lavender rickrack.
In my outfit I was sure I looked so much like Mama
her own Mama couldn't have told us apart.
I was so proud of myself I could die.
It was Mama, after all, I wanted to look like.

And all my childhood she sewed for me.
There was a fuzzy jacket one Easter
when I was about eight, the clearest robin's egg blue.
A topper, she called it;
my hatband had rosebuds on it.

There were so many dresses over the years.
Light blue organdy with a square neck and sash
for my first dance.
Later, an Easter dress of cream cotton
with neat rows of apple blossoms,
pink and green twining in the print.
Another year, a pale plaid suit in those same
soft colors.

In everything she made, I believe now I must have been beautiful.
"Now be a good girl," she would tell me,
as I put each one on, and I wanted to be that too.

Later, when I was teaching,
she sewed for me so that I would look professional.
I used to believe she was ashamed of me
because I was a terrible housekeeper
and I was afraid of babies.
I have more sense than to believe that now,
as she would say,
though I'll never forget her telling me on one visit,
"If you don't keep those baseboards cleaner,
you won't have a friend in the world!"

Without her help,
my children would have been a mess,
my dissertation unfinished,
and I would never have been able
to do what I loved in my work.

Out of dark blue velvet, wool, and cotton,
lace, denim, rayon, flannel,
my mother has sewn my life together
and taught me to make it my own.

Not only that, but Mama sewed together air and earth,
fire and water,
and she did it to the end.
She sewed her own shroud, of goodness and kindness,
with much beauty.
I see her clad now in the happy glory of God,
still sewing,
in her everlasting garment of love,
still teaching me to sew.

Today We Put Your Casket in the Ground

Mama, today we put your casket in the ground.
Artificial turf, lovely flowers that rarely grow wild,
a tent above you
and folding chairs
beside you.
It was real dirt though;
I saw a pile of it as we went through
the gates of Pythion Ridge,
and it wasn't only from your grave.

All of us die;
it's something of a comfort.
God's mercy is spread over us too;
the earth, life, and light await us.

I can trust this absolutely:
God will get it right.

Holy Thursday

It's Holy Thursday.
Twenty-two years ago on this very day Daddy died.
This afternoon was Mama's memorial service.
Holy Saturday was Daddy's funeral;
twenty-two years ago.
The whole church was white with dogwoods and lilies
for the Easter vigil.

Palm Sunday Mama died.
The funeral home, the grave, the memorial service,
beautiful too,
mostly decorated with florist flowers;
entirely filled with love.

Good Friday

Coming off the cross,
sometimes Mary holds Jesus,
sometimes Jesus holds Mary.

This year, most faithful of all who love,
hold my mother tight.
The two of you have so much in common.

Good Friday, Still

Home now to the familiar places.
It is a miracle there is still air to breathe
and ground to stand on.
I've wondered for years whether there could be.
I'm happy to report that, indeed,
there is air and ground.

Now the dog settles into his sheepskin on the couch.
Richard fusses in the kitchen,
and I sit here, still in my coat,
a bit dazed but alive,
wondering what to do with myself
now that it is seven o'clock
and there is no Mama to call,
no wrenched heart (mine)
no bewildered voice (hers)
no chest thrashing to draw in any air it can,
no shaky old legs that can barely stand,
struggling to walk on the way to bed, feeling for the floor.

Easter Saturday

Like a burn patient
I feel the pain all at once.
It comes on, intense, sudden,
hard to locate precisely,
except by the blisters and oozing,
the skin dark red and shiny.

Mama, I can't imagine the world without you.
Your love for me
(for all of us)
held us all in life—
you, me, the children,
dogs, trees, clouds,
frogs and toads,
grass, amoebas, germs,
goats, daffodils, and every spring flower.

It is not time for winter.
Tomorrow is Easter,
one week since you died.
Your children and your grandchildren
cry for you,
"Come back, come back!"
What if your love is not strong enough for us?

Tomorrow is Easter.
Like a burn patient,
will it bring some easing
to what feels like charring in the bones?

Easter

Rainy today but with buds
and the kind of soft grass
you find spring rabbits in.
Jesus is around here somewhere.
It's been a week, and Mama in my heart
is beginning to nap a little.

It's funny how the external
and internal festivals don't quite coincide.
Good Friday always feels like itself.
But Easter?
Sometimes yes and sometimes no,
and this year I can't decide,
I'm not even sure which is which.

CHAPTER
3

Family, Friends, and the Communion of the Saints

How could any of us survive our losses without each other? We can't do it, but we don't have to. I didn't always know this fact, however, and you may not have either.

I began my graduate work as a lonely person. Most of the other students were male, and they regularly informed me one way or another that I didn't belong there. My parents didn't approve, and it seemed at the time like no one else in the world did either. One night I had a short but telling dream. I dreamed that I was a star, millions of light years from earth, all by myself. I realized when I woke up that having learned about Origen, a writer of the early church who believed that the stars were alive, prompted my dream. Origen believed that stars' work in the universe came in praising

God continually. If his speculation is true, the stars may appreciate this task, but I still remember the terror and despair that dream generated in me when I looked out into black and empty space, cut off from any other living thing.

The fact is that none of us is alone. From the eighteenth century onward, modern folks have been encouraged to glorify the "self-made" person, "the rugged individualist," and the singular people who seem to have accomplished great things with no help from others. Fortunately, this way of viewing the world is fading. Most of us realize to a certain extent that we couldn't exist without one another, if only to provide us with roads, electricity, the rule of law, schools, medical help, groceries in the stores, clothes on our backs, and so forth. Real people who work in our world with us provide our necessities. But our lack of aloneness goes beyond these areas to include our spiritual and emotional lives.

A friend told me a story once while I was trying to live through a bad patch and felt close to despair. When he and his wife were young, they had wanted a baby more than anything. For years they tried, until at last, his wife was pregnant. They were happy until the baby actually arrived. From birth, it was obvious that in spite of his physical perfection something had gone awry with the baby. He couldn't stand to be touched; and as he grew, he seemed unable to connect with his parents or anybody else in any way. Of course the parents loved him and raised him as best they could. When the boy turned eighteen, he wanted to live by himself, so they set him up in a garage apartment a block from their house. From that distance they could continue to feed him, do his laundry, and care for his other needs. After six months, my friend went to check on his son one morning and found him dead. He had killed himself beside a pile of magazines with articles underlined about the hopelessness of schizophrenia, which was his diagnosis.

My friend and his wife were worse than heartbroken at the time. He didn't know how they would survive the death, but he told me how they lived through it. At the funeral, people said to him over and over, "Tom, you know your faith will get you through this." He stopped for a moment, looked at me, and then said, "Roberta, it was not *my* faith that got me through it. It was the faith of my friends."

I have never forgotten this generous sharing of his painful story at a time I needed to hear it, a time when I was not sure I could believe in much of anything positive. That I have been saved by the faith of my friends I have found to be true again when my hope, energy, and, yes, faith have failed me.

My hope, energy, and faith failed when mother was dying. I didn't think I could stand it. I couldn't bear to see her suffering, and I couldn't imagine the world with me in it without her. But my brothers and sisters-in-law were there, along with my nieces and nephew and my son. My husband and daughter called often, expressing their love. Somehow the solidness of this shared love got all of us through this period of spiritual dryness and fatigue. It was the ground under our feet and the roof over our heads. It continues to be so.

In one more place I've continued to feel sustained through this time, and all times, for that matter. I feel sustained by my strong sense of sharing in the communion of the saints from the beginning of time until now. Athanasius, the desert mothers and fathers, Julian of Norwich, my grandmother, my dear friend Sharon who came a long way with her husband to the funeral to be with me, and Ike, my friend and former student and his partner who also came, as well as so many others who could not. I felt the support not only of those I have known, loved, and trusted but also the support of human beings who do not know me personally, yet who partake in common grief and joy simply by sharing our common human lives, conditions, and experiences over the centuries. Do I need to know them to love all these people, living and dead, or to feel the love they transmitted through the medium of God in whom we all exist? I don't believe so. Love, after all, is enough.

Brothers

1.

What would the world do without brothers?
I know there are many places
women might be better off.
But in those parts of the world
husbands and fathers are problematic too,
if you happen to be female.

This is not the case with my good brothers.
If I had to have an image of these men
when my mother died,
it would be of strong branches
thin and supple, interlaced, leafy green,
creating a net beneath me
that I knew I could trust.

Love was its basic structure,
solid as earth,
real as air.

2.

My earliest memory of Fred
(the older of the two)
is of him with an ice cream cone.
He was about three years old.
The ice cream was melting
all over his face and hands
and down his clothes.
He was so serious
and so helpless in the face of all that melting.

I, the big sister, looked at him, I think,
and saw him for the first time
for what he was,
a little boy who was so vulnerable,
so fragile in his happiness
that I wanted to cry.

I wanted to forget this glimpse of him
then and later as I grew.
How can you have sibling rivalry, after all,
if your heart constricts in a knot
when you see your sibling?
How can you properly shout
and sulk, resent and pout
that you might not get your share?
But I remembered that ice cream
even though I didn't want to.

Perhaps all his grown-up goodness
was hidden in this delicate
scene of ice cream eating.
I couldn't say then or now
why it was heartbreaking,
even to remember.

I can say, I know that the tenderness of his heart,
his great love for all of us,
grows from the roots of the tree
whose branches interwoven
supported me through the worst of Mama's death.
I don't understand any of it, but I'm pretty sure it has something
to do with melting ice cream.

3.

Wes is my other brother.
Wes was the baby.
He was so cute,
I hated him for it.
There is a picture of him
in short little overalls, striped seersucker,
I believe,
in front of a bush and grinning.
It made me mad;
I was eleven years old,
and I felt sure he was looking cute on purpose.

He was the one in nursery school
the teachers loved.
He was the mischievous one
of the three of us,
a child who grinned and enjoyed himself.
Fred and I were too serious
for much fun,
I'm afraid, too serious for our own good.

But, like me, Wes has always liked old things.
He favored archeology and arrowheads;
I went for the Middle East—
Hebrew, the Egyptian desert,
Haroun al-Rashid of the Arabian nights.

Both of us valued antiques.
Whatever Wesley felt about what he loved,
for me it was the sense of joining with the long dead
through the things they cared about,
a kind of communion of the saints
where everybody is a saint by virtue of being human.
Wes has lived his professional life among these things,
beautiful things and exotic things,
handmade things, paintings, woven and cast things,

knives and guns and books.
All this is his passion.

We should have been close, he and I,
but we haven't been.

Too much distance in age and miles,
maybe too much stuff from childhood.
But he too was a strong tree of love while my mother died, root
    and branch.
Also kind and good,
his love upheld me those terrible days,
and I have probably survived.

4.

My brothers' love has surely been the love of God
poured out over all of us
like a heavy rain
soaking our hearts,
softening what is hard,
making all things grow.

I repent for the ways in which
I have nearly lost these brothers.
I vow to amend my ways.

Shelley, Here You Come

Here you come bringing your good food
for the lot of us,
lentil soup before Mama died
(she couldn't eat it, but she loved lentils)
pasta casserole later
to nourish and sustain.

You looked so pretty;
you were always pretty.
My sister-in-law,
my sister.
It comforts me to look at you.

You too cried like your heart was broken,
like the rest of us.
Our grief comforted each other.

You brought your kind and good children,
grownups for any grandmother to delight in.
Beautiful with your same dark eyes
and shiny hair.

Now you help put away Mama's things,
emptying the spaces full of her
that we must empty,
packing away forever what must go.

I know how good at this you are,
how hard and fast you work,
because you did it for me
when we left our house,
when I so needed it
and couldn't do it for myself
in a thousand years.

It is a truly cosmic skill
you own,
to disassemble and not break
what you are taking apart.
You fold things up and box them,
hands as delicate as hummingbirds
but more gentle.

Linda, There Are No Words

Linda, there are no words for you,
no syllables to use.
You were a daughter to Mama,
a Ruth to make even Ruth
look like a slacker.

It was not just at the end
you cared for her,
shopping, finding doctors
(and there were a lot),
then driving her there,
waiting and waiting,
doing her laundry
("I like to do laundry," you said).

Keeping up with her money,
paying her bills,
finding her hearing aids
(though I am sure she didn't need them
to hear your love visiting her
with your energy and kindness).

As far as I can see,
your attention and love were
always upon her,
in the face of her absent daughter.
Not my fault, but still—
you were never irritable with her.

Calm and competent as Ruth,
doing yourself what needed to be done for her.
No longer an in-law,
just like Ruth, but a true daughter
and sister as well to me.

I'm just so glad you didn't have to marry Boaz!

Offspring

Trees don't seem to have trouble
with their little seedlings,
nor have I seen one worry
about their fully grown offspring either.
How can a sweet gum make a mistake
or a hemlock speak a wounding word
that might wither its children
down to the roots?

As for me,
it's not so easy being a parent.
The hard part is where I get officious and bossy
and hurt my children's feelings.

Now I remember every disaster of their own childhood,
handled by me heavy-handed
in stupid panic,
and I continue to act just like I did then.

Forgive me, my dear children.
I would like to tell you every blunder
arose from love
but this would be a lie.
As often as not,
it was exhaustion,
desperation,
fear for you
and for me too,
that grabbed me by the throat.

I love you with every cell of my body,
and I am so sorry.

Lewis and Sharon

Last night a friend came
bringing gossip,
news of his children,
reports of the weather
in far away Durham
(three weeks of snow
and much shoveling in March).
I laugh for the first time in days
and stick my head up out of my hole
to check the weather here
where it ought to be snowing too.

"Mama, I won't abandon you," I tell her.

What kind of person am I? I wonder.
"Take any day out of hell that you can get,"
says Sharon.

I try to trust her.

Friends

I can't imagine how people get through life without friends.
I couldn't have survived without them
since the day Mama took a turn for the worse,
or even worse, a turn for the worst.

Theoretically, our souls rest in God
and this is true,
so long as we don't understand this resting
in terms of being someplace else.

In fact, our souls in pieces rest in our friends
who bear the face of God for us.
I'm pretty sure talk of the image of God
implies something like this:
Us—friends—God
Friends—us—God
Us—God—friends,
on into combinations we cannot describe
and can't recognize when we come upon them.

"But who are my friends?" I ask,
and the answer appears to be obvious.
The ones who love me,
who traveled a long way to be with me
in the face of Mama's death.
The ones who wrote to me,
the ones who didn't call when I couldn't talk,
the ones who tried to call and I couldn't talk,
the ones who sent cards
whom I barely know.
The ones who sent me love and I knew it,
also the ones who sent me love and I didn't know it.

There are special friends to whom I bow in gratitude.
But there are also friends I've never met and never will,
who bless me by their presence in the universe.

Julian of Norwich

I've been thinking a lot about you lately, Julian,
having dreamed of you,
remembering spending an evening with you at a party.
I can't think where the party was,
what city or even what country,
but I do recall the house.
It was old-fashioned in the not at all stylish way,
boxy, three-storied if you count the finished basement,
avocado appliances in the kitchen,
one bathroom for the whole place,
fixtures a bit waxy with soap residue from years of use,
thin towels, a claw-foot tub over dull linoleum.
In the other rooms, cheap wood paneling
with skinny, scuffed molding,
battered furniture, couch, too-big square coffee table, chairs.
A dining table with an old lace tablecloth,
covered with the sort of party food
people who are not really interested in eating serve their guests.

The rooms were crowded and noisy,
everyone, mostly younger people, standing,
everyone talking and having a good time,
eating off paper plates, drinking from plastic cups.

I was standing off by myself, not talking to anyone
when you came in,
and you saw me immediately.
You smiled at me and took my arm.
"Let's go downstairs where it's quieter," you said,
and so we did.

The room, more paneling on the walls, no windows,
was empty of people and quiet.
There were a couple of card tables pushed together
covered with a paper cloth.

Again, the usual food,
bowls of salted nuts, a plate of cheese and crackers,
rolled up bits of ham held together with toothpicks.

You dropped your coat on a chair and smiled at me.
"It is so good to see you," you said.
You hugged me then, and you smelled warm and womany.
"It is wonderful to see you," I answered, hugging back,
and, oh, did I mean it!

I wasn't dressed in party clothes and neither were you,
but you looked very nunny—
lace-up shoes, black polyester skirt halfway to your ankles,
some kind of a smooth brown top, rather dark,
matching something like a nun's short brown veil,
your dark brown hair poking out.

I have seen so many statues and paintings of you,
all looking elegant and spiritual and tall.
How different you looked in the flesh!
A bit on the short and heavy side.
Nobody would notice you at church or the grocery store,
an ordinary middle-aged woman,
no form of comeliness that anyone would desire you.
No vanity in you at all.
("Of course there is," you say now,
"I am human, aren't I?")

I wanted to be in your presence more than anything.
I was so glad.
With you, it felt like being home,
where I belonged,
good food, sound sleep, cheerful,
with an ordinary, delightfully comfortable God.
(Can I say this and not offend?)

We talked that night about everything of an everyday nature,
grocery shopping,

what was going on at the church in Norwich,
the weather,
the beauty of the day,
the children who came in and out of our lives.
A little bit about spiritual topics,
but only a little,
because it felt like every topic
we chatted about together
was a spiritual topic when it was
with you. That's just the way it was between us.

We didn't discuss why you were away from your anchorhold,
and I still don't know why—
probably something to do with God sending you to me
to save me in my very ordinary life.
It didn't feel like that though.
Rather, it was more like
two old friends, happy together in themselves.

After that dream I only saw you once in the flesh again,
but that is another story.
You went back to the fourteenth century
and I went home,
my heart happy and full of all good things,
and I suspect yours was too.
You are gone, but we are still at home together.

Time and Memory

*ime, memory, and their workings have always puzzled me, even as a small child. I believed that no event was real until the moment the person who lived through it remembered it. (It never occurred to me that I had lived through unremembered things like my own birth.) *How was it possible*, I wondered, *to die, to go from something to nothing?* Something in my heart makes me wonder about it even now. This matter of going from something to nothing continues to give me pause about time and memory.

There is another matter that I have been unable to find my way through as an adult as well as a child and has served as the source of much pondering. *Where does the past go once it is past, or is it ever really past?* Recently, for example, I have been vividly remembering the way I once experienced life with my parents. Looking back now, I would have to say that it seems to me that for good or ill, we existed together within an impenetrable and absolutely indestructible force field that could never be breached and that I could never escape. I would have to obey my parents until I died. My parents' divorce when I was twelve did not destroy the power of the force field—it stayed as real and solid as stone. Yet, with my father's death, the power of the force field lessened. I felt relieved and confused at the same time.

Now, my mother's death has come, and I find myself puzzled ten times over. I wonder, *Is that force field really gone with their deaths, and if it is, where could something that seemed so solid, so indestructible to a child's heart, have gone?* My memories of my mother in particular places doing particular things at particular times are so vivid that I can't believe they have simply died with her. The times spent with her, with me resentful and sullen, in my grandmother's kitchen in Union County, Kentucky. Her stories of picking blackberries as a child with her sister; the stories of life in the House on the Hill in which she was born; the dinners she prepared and the table I grouchily set as a teenager for my aunts and great-aunts when they would visit in Louisville. The very smells of her and the places she inhabited cannot be gone. If they remain so intensely alive in me now, then they are somewhere.

Grief distorts time like a crazy mirror. It makes the present go slowly when you want it to speed up, and it removes the barrier between now and then. What was once hazy in memory comes back in the present as sharp as a knife blade.

As for where the past goes, puzzle over it as I may, I will not know in this life. I am sure, however, that all of it is held safe and whole forever, as we are ourselves, in the living memory of God.

Ninetieth Birthday Party

For her ninetieth birthday,
six years ago,
Mama wanted a bash for a party,
to be held at her retirement home
in the big room with the pretty floor.
So she made her list of guests
and they were invited.
Most accepted.
Mama had new clothes,
a sweater with a long skirt,
(though she had wanted
something short
to be more stylish).
Linda arranged for the food
and the flowers, of course,
as she always arranged everything—beautifully.
What a blessing!

Then it was the day of the party.
We were all present from out of town
down to the last doting grandchild.

For Mama it was really too much.
She had been mopey a lot of the day already.
"What's the matter, Mama?"
I asked her.

Sitting in her blue chair,
she started to cry.
"I should have invited my cousins from Casey County,"
she answered.
Her old voice was full of anguish.
"I used to play with them when I was a little girl!"
she whispered.

Then I was full of anguish too.
Poor Mama.
Oh, Mama!
Were these cousins still children together
in her mind?
Playing house and chasing each other
over the grass,
and hiding in the barn?

In actual fact,
were they all dead now, anyway?
I had never heard of them before,
but clearly, they were as fresh and present
to her as the morning sun on a bright day.

But the sun was almost gone now,
and Mama had been left behind
in the growing darkness, cousin-less.

Mortality.
This means Mama suffering,
old and bewildered,
me, now and then in anguish for her, still,
in spite of the kindness of God,
in anguish for us all.

This Is What I Am Pondering Today

This is what I am pondering today:
It is the experience of time.
This is the fifth month since Mama died
and something terrible has happened to the clock.
The hours pass more quickly than I ever remember.
By the time I have finished breakfast
and contemplated God and loved all those I love
and those I try to love,
lunch has come.
I scrounge up something—
leftovers if I am lucky,
but probably peanut butter on stale crackers
or a bit of cottage cheese that's been around too long—
I eat, then
I throw out my trash and rinse my plate,
fool around doing nothing,
and then I weave.
The threads shine, going in and out,
the cloth builds.
A few minutes later, it is time for dinner.
I eat again, talk on the phone, walk my dog,
and it's time for bed.
That's my day, gone before I've really gotten up.

As for my weeks and my months—
they whip by so fast
they blow my hair back from my face
and make my eyes water.
I miss appointments,
which can't have come already.
I forget what I am doing when I blink.
I watch the hair on my little white dog grow
from morning till night—

or is it from minute to minute in these quick hours?
This wind blows on him too,
small and vulnerable as he is,
and soon it will be winter.

I am happy now but I feel the cold coming.
I weave and my hip hurts from sitting.
The leaves on the dogwoods
and the maples
are only now fully out,
and they are already faintly splashed with red.

What shall I do, or can I do anything at all,
or do I even want to?
Time and grief, grief and time;
like everything else on this green planet,
they are
in the hands of God
but inexplicable.

Time Was Always Rushing You Away

Today, Mama, I am wondering again about
your conviction that time was always rushing you away
or at least toward somewhere
you weren't prepared to go.
"It's going to be Christmas before you know it,"
you would sigh in the middle of August,
reproaching me for something,
I never knew what.

What I do know now is that what made the world solid
when I was a child
was the existence of my great-grandmother, Grammar,
and Papa, my great-grandfather,
and Papa Charles and Panny, my grandparents,
and my great-aunts and great-uncles,
and my aunts and uncles too,
and cousins in every combination,
and of course, you, my Mama
all in a lump with no cracks or corners.

I believed in the pit of my stomach
there was no way for anybody to die out of it,
or even leave to go on a long trip
to some place unimaginable,
without something even more unimaginable
happening to the entire universe.

On the other hand,
I remember you telling stories in Panny's kitchen,
cooking and washing dishes
with my great-aunt Nacky and my aunts and Panny,
stories of your own great-grandmother,
Grandma Nack (mean as a snake, I concluded),
and your great-aunts and cousins

and great-uncles and grandfathers and grandmothers
and I knew that, while no one could leave the lump by dying
(once you were in, you were in),
all these relatives were, in fact, mostly, impossibly, dead.

No wonder you couldn't trust time,
that you always sighed in summer,
"You wait and see,
it will be winter before you know it."

On the other hand, Mama, the impossible thing
for the child I was
was this:
The combined lives seemed so solid,
so all of a piece,
your stories so closely fitted together,
there seemed to be no room for the small
and alien person I was at all.

Blackberries

To my knowledge I never ate
a blackberry pie that Mama made.
This was a shame.

Mama was a cook like you wouldn't believe.
You name it, Mama could cook it,
and everyone would be dying to eat it.

Biscuits, heavenly.
Rolls, tears to the eyes.
But piecrust!
Nothing was as good as that.

When we were growing up,
she would make fruit pies
with latticework tops,
cherry for George Washington's birthday,
apple from Panny's June apple tree,
and peach from the peach trees
in Panny's chicken yard when we were there.

She only used the ones that
fell to the ground, bruised or rotten.
A nasty feeling under the feet,
that chicken yard.
The outhouse was at the back of it and
it was hard in childhood
to separate peaches from chickens pecking,
chicken poo,
peaches from wet feathers,
peaches and the smell of lime.
Disgusting!

But I digress.
It was that piecrust we were talking about.
She used lard to make it flaky
when we were little.
This was before the invention
of hydrogenated cooking oil, I would guess.
Maybe not, though
she might have just pooh-poohed it
since her grandmother wouldn't have used it,
since it wasn't real.

Oh, that crust was something!
She would chop that lard into the flour and salt
with a pair of forks,
make it into two balls,
roll it out with a rolling pin on waxed paper,
and cut out circles of it to fit the pan.

Unbaked, it was the color of raw linen.
Baked, it was surely the golden color
of wheat in heaven.

Best of all, whenever she would make it,
she would cut the leftover dough in strips
to bake in another pan
along with the pie.

This was the children's part, and it came out first.
The smell, slightly salty, toasty,
a little floury and lardy,
full of small layers of air,
a perfect, light crunch.
I would always burn myself on it.
I would make an arch with the top of my mouth
to get all the taste out of it.
"Disgusting!" Mama would say. "How greedy you are.
Ladies don't act like that!"

But she never made a blackberry pie though
she told me enough times how
ripe blackberries marked her childhood days in July.
The family lived next to a small woods that were full of them.

Panny would give Mama and little Aunt Kas pails
to bring home full for pies.
She always did her part, Mama would say,
and fill her bucket in the dark under the trees.
But, she would add indignantly right up to the end,
Aunt Kas would always eat more than she ever brought home.

I never did find out how many pies there would be
by the time they were all through.
There would have been a lot of chigger bites though,
and scratches and ant bites and stings.

When my brothers and I would visit Panny
in the western Kentucky summers,
we would go out to do our picking
just like Mama had done.
Of course, it wasn't the same.
It was a different, smaller woods by then
and twenty-five years later.
The chiggers were fiercer,
the scratches deeper,
and the berries more mythical than not.

But Mama had picked them
so we wanted to do it too.
It was like doing something concrete
to prove the existence of fairies.
Mama was a child once?
If we did what she had done,
we might be able to believe it.

Mamas were magical to us in those days.
Secretly huge, they filled the sky.

And they must have lived since creation.
They must still be like this to children.
("Mama, when you were a little girl,
did they have cooked food?"
my little boy once asked me.
"Sometimes," I told him.)

No blackberry pies for my brothers and me.
In our time, they were almost imaginary.
Or rather, they were like mead
or ambrosia
or any other of those foods
eaten only by the long-dead gods.

Nobody ate them any longer,
we finally came to know.
Nevertheless,
if anyone could bake them still,
it would have been our Mama.

Today at the End of Rain

Driving to Louisville today,
heavy and sad to pack up your things,
the traffic was terrible.
It thumped and poured from Nashville on.

In the car I nodded on and off.
In those hours
memories of childhood rains
came to me so strongly,
I had no sense of time past or present.
There I was, hiding in Papa Charles's red barn,
rain pinging on the roof of the hayloft,
the smell of grasses
gold and pale green,
dried and bundled, ready to eat.
(Perhaps I was a cow,
which smelled so good,
so safe and sleepy.)

But there was also rain in the chicken yard,
hitting the dirt in small circles,
and a peculiar smell of rotten peaches.

This was the rain we drove through
late this afternoon.
I was still in the barn,
still with the chickens
(there were sweet peas
and orange cowslips on my grandmother's fence)
but also, I was somewhere else. The fat rain
hit a hot road and sizzled,
a summer smell like no other,
one every child knows.

In each present memory, Mama,
you are there,
one rain after another,
not just in childhood
but through a lifetime,
but also all at once.

Tonight, after dinner we were glad to be together.
We walked outside and found
the rain was over.
We saw the sky, deep blue to our left,
luminous pink and peach to our right.

And arching over everything,
illuminating roofs and trees,
telephone wires
and the birds sitting on them,
lightening all hearts and hurts,
laughing and praying in every color,
was a perfect rainbow.

The Burden of Your Sadness

I think the burden of your sadness
has dropped off me.

From the time I was a little girl
it has been like clothes to me,
freezing my skin
and weighing a hundred pounds,
shirts, underwear, dresses, sweater,
cotton socks
all soaked in icy rain.

I've wondered where it came from,
that sucking melancholy.
It seems that it was there long before my father
left you.
Perhaps it was gloom from my grandmother
for whom I am named.
All those miscarriages over the years,
punctuated by seven live births.
One baby lost.

Panny's own disappointment,
her impossible father,
no money—
who knows.

I just know how it is with mothers and daughters
as far back as I can see.
Can't tell where one starts and the last one ends.
Can't tell whose memory it is,
yours or hers back forever.
Sometimes it's the communion of the saints,
sometimes communion of the sinners,
time dissolved and run together.

What I do know specifically about you and me, Mama,
is that it was my responsibility
to ease myself under your load to carry with you
what you couldn't bear alone.
You never told me so in just these words;
you may not know you told me at all.
Daddy's desertion,
shame over being divorced at a time nobody divorced,
pride
and your own Mama's grief on top of it.

It's been too much for me to bear.
Whatever its origins, I couldn't put it down
and leave you crushed beneath it.

For now, it's gone,
gathered by the river;
it's dropped off both of us.

I can only hope it is not creeping around
looking for my daughter,
your granddaughter,
speaking in a new tongue,
tearing up, whining to her, and lying,
unknown to me as it was to you,
"Pick me up; your Mama needs you.
Pick me up,
your grandmother needs you too."

Household Goods

*T*here is something about the things those we love have made with their own hands or used or even valued. When I fell in love with my husband, I delighted in the items he gave me that had been his: a piece of wood he had carved as a boy and an ivory tusk off some unidentifiable animal—both perfectly worthless, true, but providing a physical link between him and me when he wasn't with me. The gifts he has given me over the years still act this way, bringing much comfort while he is many miles away at his work.

The little clothes I've saved, the Christmas ornaments the children made in school years ago, the handprints in clay carefully painted, my daughter's pictures of happy or mischievous animals doing outrageous things, the cup my son brought me from a trip he took—all these are precious to me. These physical things don't just *remind* me of the children; they *connect* me to them—and keep me connected.

Though my two sisters-in-law did most of the work of it, dismantling Mama's little apartment after she died was agonizing. The place was full of beautiful things she had bought or been given from antique stores over the years (an item that had been loved by someone else was always better than something perfect and anonymously new). She kept the things she inherited from people she loved, right down to pictures on the walls, rugs on the floor, silver in her kitchen drawers, and quilts in her closet. She had a few things that had come to her from her own mother, who never had much—but nothing from her grandmother and only a few things from her aunts. Much that filled her apartment came from her sisters, her children, her daughters-in-law, her children's children, her cousins' children, and her nieces and nephews. We uncovered a lot of beloved stuff the children had made her over the years: construction-paper creations by five-year-olds, handmade birthday cards, a little stained-glass window made by a niece, children's presents from a dollar store, dishes and antique lamps bought on trips she had taken with the various women of the family she loved so well. None of this even begins to include the possessions she had that reminded her of her own happy childhood. Everything she had used for cooking and cleaning was full of her and her memories. In fact, the whole place was full of the power of her love.

So the job of dismantling was a terrible one. It was made far less terrible by the fact that after all the children and grandchildren selected what they wanted of her possessions, almost nothing was left that had mattered to her. Her children loved her. Her grandchildren adored her. Now her things—down to the last paperweight—surround them. All of us are connected to her through objects in a very physical way.

No wonder relics of the saints have been venerated and loved by many Christians over the centuries. Though the idea of their bones being holy and powerful is alien and perhaps even repulsive to many people, to me the urge to venerate the physical remains of these special people and to call on their power for blessing makes as much sense to my heart as pondering the words of the books many of them have written.

We are spiritual beings without any doubt, but the physical is not actually the opposite of spiritual. We can love the particular things of this material life as we love the bodies of our dear ones. They connect us, carrying our very selves along with our memories, to those who are physically gone from our lives. They remind us all of our very real place in the communion of the saints.

I do not find it surprising that sleeping under one of Mama's quilts in my own bed at night makes me feel her arms around me, loving me still, reminding me that I am safe in the universe.

Today We Packed Up

It wasn't something I wanted,
to go through Mama's things,
dividing them up,
packing them up in anonymous cardboard boxes,
throwing away, giving away,
storing away, saving for her grandchildren.
But Mama wasn't there
and she didn't care what we were doing.
In fact, from far away she called to us,
(she must be traveling at the speed of light
 to have gotten that far already)
"You children don't worry so much about that stuff.
It's just stuff."

This certainly didn't sound like our mother,
so we called back as loudly as we could,
"These things were yours and you loved them.
How can you say to us now, just don't worry about them?"

"I can say it if I want to," you answered us.
"I can feel any way I want to."

Now, we really were struck dumb
by such an out-of-character reply.

But then, to make matters worse,
while we were still silent and looking at each other,
she went on.
"I don't want to hear the three of you fighting.
Just be sweet to each other,
you hear?"

At this, we could hardly think of what to say:
We were already so glad to be together,
we were just wiggling.

A Storm Last Night

A storm last night,
booms of thunder,
the smells of spring rain.
This morning drops of water
caught on the baby
sweet gum leaves,
little windows, perfectly clean
(unlike my own)
but not transparent.

So, what does that rain
have to do with Mama now?

A blue bowl
bought at a dollar store.
She is cutting up fruit
for a salad,
apples and peaches,
melon and oranges,
and the dreaded banana
(it always went slimy on the second day).

I see the juice in the bottom
of the bowl
against that blue,
like the drops on the gum leaves,
murky but Mama's.
Each fruit salad my whole life
has been Mama's,
and I suppose it always will be.

But why do I have to remember
where every little thing
she owned
came from?

Dollar stores, her sister,
her aunt, her children,
grandchildren, friends.
There are paperweights, jackets,
pillows for the couch,
shoes and plates,
the stockings in her drawer,
the earrings she once wore,
undershirts, a robe.

Delicate and bewildered like a child,
the fruit salad standing for who knew what,
she longed to feed us,
and she couldn't.
A cut glass bowl
couldn't save her,
and neither could we comfort her.

Loss

*N*ot many things in life are more painful than the knowledge that the people we have loved and still love are absolutely gone from this earth. We will never again hear their voices, never touch them or be touched by them, see their faces, or feel the weight of their bodies against ours. The structure of our world and their solid place in it has come apart, and nothing fits together anymore. The pieces overlap where they didn't before, and great gaping holes with jagged edges surface and it seems we can never fill them. This was my sense of things when my father died and my beloved aunt and doubly so at the death of Mama.

The conviction that all things are held safely in God, as I believe; or that God will finally restore all our losses and wipe away every tear from every eye, which with Julian of Norwich I also believe; that nothing God has created is ultimately lost—none of these beliefs relieves the pain. We are animals with animal bodies as well as spirits, and we are our bodies. We may not like them when we suffer in them, but they are ours. As the early church meant to recognize when it affirmed the resurrection from the dead, we belong in our bodies and so do all those other human beings we love or have loved. Faith doesn't ask us to give up this conviction in favor of a more cheerful view of their loss in the worst of our suffering; it supports us through it.

I don't believe it helps to tell ourselves or others that since God is good, "everything happens for a reason." Of course, it does. If God created all that exists, then nothing is truly random. But what is the reason for what happens? Aside from our negligence or ignorance or an accident or whatever, we simply can't grasp why some things happen, no matter how much we long to understand. It doesn't ease the pain to tell ourselves or others that "God needed her more than I did," or, as is sometimes said at a child's funeral, "God took her to be a little flower on his desk." What kind of God do we worship, praise, and serve if that is our understanding and belief?

I offer this truth: People die because God gave us life and made us mortal. Being mortal means we will inevitably suffer and die. As Jesus tells Julian of Norwich in one of her visions, "Know that whatever you do, you will have woe," because it is the nature of all human life. We are mortal, and we always will be. Is it anybody's fault that this is true? No, says Julian, not God's and not ours either.

The desolation of loss simply comes with being human. The women at the Crucifixion must have agonized over Jesus' suffering, just as the mothers of any suffering children go through crushing grief on their behalf. None of the disciples, except for John, could stand to be at the foot of the cross at all.

Desolation is a part of loss. Pretending it is not may give some temporary relief. But I wonder if we can find any consolation ultimately if we don't first allow ourselves to feel it in all its awfulness. We may have to rail against God or against the universe, lie down on the floor and howl, or cry until our eyes are dry. We might have to allow desolation to wholly consume us for a time. We walk on our pilgrimage through the bitter valley until, improbable as it may seem, it becomes for us a pool of blessings.

Every Evening About Now

Every evening about now
it was our custom, Mother's and mine,
that I should call her,
which I did, after the dog ate
and before I ate
and before she went to bed.

It wasn't very much of a span of time I had
to catch her between her evening meal and sleep,
so I got up from the table in restaurants,
and stood outside movie theatres,
and stopped my weaving,
got myself home from walking the dog,
found places in retreat centers that had reception,
interrupted tense conversations with the children,
startled from a late nap
to catch her while she could still hear me
before she took her hearing aids out and fell asleep.

It was a painful time of day
to hear Mama, night after night, declining
and be able to do nothing but suffer with her.
It hurt to the soul,
like a knife from belly to throat.
It made my body weak,
and it wasn't so great for my mind either.
I often had trouble paying attention
when people talked to me,
and I couldn't remember what to do
when directions were given to me
for doing difficult things,
like how to turn on the TV
or where to take the car to change the oil.

Now I plan my day around this familiar time,
but there is no call to make.
Mama is not suffering, true,
and I am very glad—happy even,
but I still can't pay attention when I am spoken to
more often than not,
and I now recall that I have never in my life
remembered directions.

I am worse than forgetful these days,
six weeks after.
Perhaps it's dementia of my own.
I surely feel demented.
I stare at her blue bathrobe
behind the bathroom door
and see her poor body,
wrinkled and creased,
as she struggles
to find where to put her arms.

Still, progress is being made toward summer.
The white and yellow daisies are beginning,
and the mountain laurel buds are getting ready
for what they will do in a week or two.
Yesterday I saw a solitary Indian paintbrush
blooming red amongst the rocks,
the ponds and rivers are full of water
to make things grow.

And I am grateful, and gratitude itself
is a gift greater than all these others.
Mother isn't suffering,
and I rest from the phone calls
and wait for the end of restlessness.

I feel her closeness and I hear her voice.
Still, I miss her.

The Memory of Scents

It is a sunny day, trees half in leaf,
the green of nothing but themselves.
I walk the road.
Sometimes the dog's behind me,
sometimes in front,
sniffing the ground loudly
for fox and deer.
That he would come upon one or the other
is my worst fear.
He's very small and white,
and he doesn't know to be afraid.

The smell of cut lumber comes to me,
the scent of wisteria follows me everywhere,
freshly laundered sheets
(*where are they?* I wonder)
and crushed leaves, sweet like grass,
but with a bitter aftertaste.

I lost my sense of smell and taste
for five whole years once,
and it's never come completely back.
It's amazing how memory is stored
in what we smell,
how our own history even from childhood is
hidden in suddenly recalled flavors.
Taste and smell—they hold our continuity,
girl to woman, city child to country,
and back again.
They hold our pain too
and carry it for us when we least want it.
The odd scent
of my father's body in the mornings,
long gone now, but he was too, even in my childhood.

Mother smelled of good things cooking,
baking things and meat with garlic,
summer dinners with the back door open.

Also, the odor of fresh laundry hung out to dry in the sun.
Seersucker pajamas were the best.
There was the smell of wet clothes going through
the wringer that sat above the round tub
on grey legs in the kitchen.
I was two years old and couldn't resist that wringer
with the chair next to it.
(Wrung-out fingers felt nothing like I expected.)
So many tastes and smells, my mother.

Mama is gone now,
and no scent of her remains
except the scents of ordinary life,
only the scents by which I orient myself
in a dark room,
by which I tell the inside from the out,
and go to church,
and know to shop
to feed the children,
to dress myself,
and lie down to sleep,
to wake in the morning
and walk the dog.

Every scent of her
is itself a prayer.

Whether Report

Tonight:
Downcast skies, low pressure center,
chilly with an eighty percent chance of showers.
The outlook for later in the week:
Expect more of the same.
Cold, rain, plenty of chance of rain,
whether or not we do a thing.

Mama, I Don't Know

Mama, I don't know what the heck I'm doing.
I miss you,
I feel so scattered, so absentminded,
hungry and nauseous,
a bit depressed, at loose ends.
I want to stay in bed
but I'm too restless to do it.
Even the dog paces around,
then goes to sleep on the sofa.

I'm still not weaving—
That takes such internal organization,
threads, structures, colors, loom,
it wears me out to think about it.
I am sure God's telling me to tough it all out,
but I can't imagine doing it.
I need my brothers and
I need a whole lot of whining and sniveling,
not to mention self-pity.

I tell you what, Mama.
Have you ever considered coming back to us?

Not So Great Today

Today is tough.
I am so tired I could lie down in the road
and wait for a truck.
The sky is the color
of soft grey pillows.
Owls have nothing on me
when it comes to sleepy
in the daytime.

I know this is grief,
but I don't have to like it.
Just let me take a nap.
Please, just let me take a nap.

Is It True What They Say?

Is it true what they say about grief,
that it is the most self-centered of the emotions?
If it is, it's bad enough to have to grieve
without having to feel like a narcissistic drama queen
on top of it.

Be a good girl, Mama used to say.
Under the present circumstances
it is hard to know exactly how.
Anxiety is pretty self-centered too,
and I have enough of that right now
to wipe out the whole southeastern
part of the country in one blow.

The only antidote I've found to grief
is work—work and walking the dog.
The trouble is, right now,
I'm too anxious to concentrate on work,
and there's no walking the dog this morning:
It's raining out.

Who Will Call Me Dear One?

But who will call me dear one,
now that you are gone?

The night before,
there was the fiercest storm,
lightning, thunder, waterfalls of water,
gullies running full.
Last night, gentle rain—
gentle, but through all the dark hours,
soft as anything.

Today the trees are greener than ever.
This seems to happen in the spring
after such storms as these:
The colors vibrate.

Today there are more flowers than two days ago,
some I've never seen before,
in every color made brighter by the rain,
against the dark woods.

As for the thrift of yesterday,
the thrift is fading now,
the exuberant pink blossoms
knocked down by the rain.

And I still hear your voice, Mama,
but my ears strain after it.
"Now save your money," you whisper,
your voice rustling.
"Now save your money."

What a message with which to pierce a heart!
What a way to call me dear one.

Two Weeks and a Day

Two weeks and a day
since you finally boarded.
By this time,
we had been with you a week
as you gasped and heaved
to catch that train.
We ran behind you through the station,
not so out of breath as you,
but we would have been,
if we could have,
if it would have eased you.

Today I'm restless,
anxious too, as I always am
when an overnight visitor leaves.
I'm not so good at saying
good-bye and meaning it.

And you weren't even the guest.
It was I who came into your world.
How is it that you are the one who left?

Or maybe you were the one visiting,
but who received you when you got here?

I really do know, of course,
that the same one who first welcomed you
into this world
has already met you at the other end.

All mysterious, wonderful, and also blessed,
the smells of diesel, very early spring,
the sounds of the station.

Mostly, I remember
and will no doubt always remember,
your gasping,
your shoulders coming right off the bed
as you tried to breathe.
You needed to catch that train,
we all knew it.

Still, you've left us without you
to stop at the store,
to pick up some groceries,
to fill the car with gas,
to survive a traffic jam,
all ordinary things,
once we turn to go home.
Of course we know we will see you soon,
each in our own time.
But, Mama,
it is so very disorienting now.

Gone

My mother is gone.
She is not in her old apartment.
She is not at my grandmother's farm.
She is not quilting at church.
She is not struggling to get to her book club.
She is not loving on her grandchildren,
nor is she baking a pie or cooking a chicken.

She is not at work in her garden.
She is not picking flowers from the side of the road for her table.
She is not watering her plants
or hanging out laundry.

She is not asleep in the upstairs bedroom.
She is not rocking on the porch
or dusting her baseboards.
She is not polishing anything
or ironing anything either.

She is not being embarrassed by her various children's successes
or trying to sort out how to be proud of them.
She is not worn out or impatient with herself.
She is not despairing over being old.

She is not fretting about money and whether she will run out.
She is not worried for her sisters and brother.
She is not struggling to see or hear or understand.

Mama is gone.
She is not away on a trip.
She is not in a coma.
She is gone.

How can the world stand without my mother?
Why don't the mountains fall into the ocean?
Why does the rain come down?

Why is there oxygen still in the air?
Leaves on the trees?

Mama is in God,
I know it and trust it,
but Mama is not here
and I am in a panic.
I really want my mother.
I want my mother.

Healing Begins

*I*t's a funny thing about grief: healing starts at the very point where we begin to need it; that is, at the beginning of losing the person we love. When we begin to grieve, we begin to heal—even if we don't want to heal because it seems self-centered or callous. Speaking from my own experience, we can't even start to heal if we are doing our best to feel nothing at all or nothing positive at all. Perhaps we tell ourselves that our loss is not so terrible since it is God's will. Or we try to convince ourselves of our happiness for the one who died because of her vast suffering. In that case, our grieving would actually appear selfish.

Mama was two days short of ninety-six when she died. About a week before her death all the family members realized what was happening, including Mama herself. I flew to Louisville in a distraught state when my brother called me, full of nothing but fear and anxiety. When I arrived and saw her, my mind and heart immediately set off together on the journey of grief and healing that may never be fully over.

The beginning of my grief came in actually seeing Mama for myself, witnessing her suffering, and recognizing how difficult living had become for her. Her mild dementia had progressed to the point that the connections in her brain that allowed for body control and speech began to snap. Grief hit me so hard that my legs wouldn't hold me. At the same time, my love for Mama almost overwhelmed me. In the following days I found myself intensely focusing on her. I also noticed everything around me no matter how small. My love for her flowed through me and out upon her so strongly it was almost painful. It felt like the early stages of love or when my heart almost exploded with joy at the first sight of my babies—a kind of ecstasy of love and longing for Mama of the same kind.

Being flooded with almost hallucinatory memories became part of the beginning of healing too. As Mama lay there and I looked at her poor face and she looked back at me, memories came flooding back to me: How pretty she was when she was young and laughing and how stern and sad after she and Daddy divorced. I recalled walks in the park when I was twelve but also so many instances as a child when I had been angry with her. I remembered what she loved and hated, how she was with her own beloved Mama, aunts, and sisters back in Union County where we first went when we moved to Kentucky. I recollected everything in the most intimate details—from canning tomatoes in the sweaty heat to finding her when I was a teenager, tired and doing laundry on Saturdays when I got up. I remembered her going to church, shopping, cooking, quilting, cleaning, reading, studying, cuddling children, sewing, taking care of me as I finished a dissertation, and generally keeping house for me. I found it painful to remember these activities and feelings, yet the memories filled me then and fill me now with an overwhelming sense of gratitude.

Perhaps this gratitude carried the beginning of the healing of grief with it. I do not recall having ever been so completely grateful for my mother's life, her being, or her gifts in this way. It was like sunlight on a warm field, a hot meal in a safe place on a cold day, a soaking in of summer beauty complete with a breeze. It involved the limbering up of stiffened muscles, the waking from sleep. Gratitude works like this.

I didn't experience gratitude solely with respect to my mother at that time. I was full to the brim with it toward my brothers and sisters-in-law, my son and daughter, my nieces and nephew, toward the women who cared for Mama in her assisted living home, toward the men who opened the door and the women who sat at the desk, toward her friends, her minister, people in the grocery store, my own friends at home and with me. All this was healing balm to my hurting heart, and it still is.

If gratitude ushers in healing, how do we come by it? The gift of gratitude, while wonderful, is exactly that—a gift. None of us can will it into being or perform exercises to make it happen. It is a gift of God, pure grace. I do believe, however, that we will finally receive it if we look around, hold ourselves open to it, watch for it without cynicism or bullying of the universe, and long for it as best we can from the place of grief where we find ourselves.

At times it is harder to long for gratitude than at others. During these times of drought in the heart, we can still make an effort: We can try our best to long to be able to long for it, to long to long, as we hope for hope when hope is hard. "Ask, and you will receive" was spoken for us. It applies right here.

Two Weeks Later

Two weeks ago today, it was Palm Sunday,
when you died.

Mama, the longer ago it is,
the stronger my sense of you becomes,
not old and miserable as you were
but laughing
about something or other
with pure delight.

I never remember you laughing much
over the years,
but you must have laughed,
my memory of you doing it
is so vivid.

You are younger than I now,
a young woman full of good things,
enjoying everything all over the place.
I don't understand it,
but I know it.

And,
just as your sadness made me sad
(and it truly did as far back as I can remember),
I imagine your joy and those big eyes of yours
will stay with me
until I die.

My serious Mama—
you, laughing and laughing
in pure delight.
What a gift to give me!

On the Road to Cherry Log

On the road from Ellijay to Cherry Log,
where I live in the mountains
eleven miles away,
the scenery is much the same—
pine trees, some hardwoods, cedar, roads and fences,
other cars, trucks.

I keep track of where I am on the road by the landmarks.
First, the gravel company,
then the mysterious technology building,
then the car auction with the garbage dump behind it.
A certain mailbox close to an almost junkyard,
at last, a pretty little farm before my turn.

I nearly always see the not-so-pretty markers
as I drive by;
they're dreary, really,
and hurt your eyes if you look too long.

But suppose I look instead
to the spaces in between,
to where the clouds hang down in streamers in the morning,
where the trees hold up the sky,
dark green or black or pale brown,
red too, some of them, all different this time of year,
and daffodils and dandelions along the road.

All this is beautiful
without the landmarks
and even they have a beauty of their own
placed next to growing things.

And so I think,
suppose I try
to keep track of where I am in time

without the markers in my life, mostly ugly,
mostly painful things that stand out to direct me on my road,
things of childhood and youth,
grownup things, that hurt me and left their scars on me.

These are not the only things that happened.
Suppose I look at what does not stand out,
the trees and daffodils, sky, and every pretty thing.

But what if I get lost? I ask myself.
And I answer myself, *Who cares?*
There's time enough for everything.

Hearing Aids

On Monday, for the first time ever,
I got a pair of hearing aids.
This was a momentous event,
a rite of passage
comparable to my first bra
or my first high heels.
Two days short of a month since Mama died,
it marked the end of childhood,
and about time too,
since I am seventy-one, myself,
and moving to the top of the hill.

And I can hear now
things I haven't heard for years,
if I ever heard them at all—
layers of sound in bird calls,
songs with shape to them,
shiny surfaced, dark blue at the core,
maroon closer to the edges
and rich like salted butter,
smooth, like melting chocolate.
Tasted, seen, rubbed against the skin,
dissolved on the tongue,
full of joy,
overflowing as it melts on hands and face
and even feet.

Other sounds too, more than I can name.
I am hearing in three dimensions now
and even more,
sounds are coming to me on the diagonal,
in spirals, in parallel lines,
like roads on a map, rivers through a forest,
sunlight through air,

connecting all I hear,
tying me down or up
into the fact of things.

I am not talking here about the songs that seem to sing themselves
somewhere inside me, below my immediate awareness,
without my choice, even against my will
as I read the paper,
walk the dog, eat with Richard,
fold laundry, talk to friends—
a hateful hymn or a Civil War marching song
or a commercial for something nearly unspeakable.

I suppose I mean the music of the spheres:

Through one layer of ourselves
and down through all the rest
to the very bottom of our being.
After all,
we live our lives
bound to each other
through all times
in ways we can't imagine
like atoms in a molecule.

Our bindings are still there,
sound and colors,
shape and texture,
even when we can't hear them.
Hearing aids help perceive them,
and as I have also learned,
so does grief.

Lady in Red

There is a hydrangea by our front porch,
all in bloom, a lace hydrangea.
Its blossoms are blue,
the outside petals pale and delicate,
the lacy centers quivering with buds
and little hairs, fuzzy parts in a much deeper
but altogether wonderful color.

Pretty as it is,
the bush leaves me bemused;
it is like nothing I expected
when I bought it five years ago.
It was called "Lady in Red"
and red, even if it was dusty looking, is what it was.
Not pink or purple or blue or even white at all.
I was delighted by its color.

It was in the ground one year before.
I suppose it had repented of whatever made it red.
The next time it bloomed, it was in a white so virginal
it could have been in a bride's bouquet.
I could hardly believe it,
but what I believed was irrelevant to
what had happened.
The red was gone,
and it was gone for good.
For the next three years, for whatever reason, my Lady in Red
wore nothing but white.

Then, when its new flowers appeared this June,
they were no longer white,
but blue as a little boy's baby blanket,
bluer than the sky on a bright morning,
even bluer than my long-ago bewildered heart.

Nothing stays the same,
and it oughtn't to either
if its basic stuff remains.
I ought to know;
I'm such a hydrangea myself
but with my colors in a different order:
First, a dirty white,
then long years of crushing blue,
(not beautiful at all on the bush I was).
At last, in my later years, I find myself turned red,
a long-awaited, unrestrained and happy red,
still who I am,
but full now of unrepentant joy,
full of red delight.

Mama, Look Up!

On Saturday and Sunday it rained.
It rained so hard that if water had been grass,
they could have baled it for hay.

Now the flowers are really coming on.
I've seen white violets so tiny that
ten would fit on a thumbnail,
little blue flowers like forget-me-nots
so small, not much more is visible
than four minute petals and a yellow dot in the middle.

Behind a neighbor's house
amazing lady slippers bloom pink
as they wait for feet to come and try them on,
around dead stumps in the scraggly woods.

Rhododendrons are opening magenta blooms now
the size of grapefruit.
Buttercups shine so yellow that butter is embarrassed,
and the little wild strawberry blossoms
copying the buttercups,
shout, Look at me! I'm yellow too!

Best of all is the moss this year.
It is so thick, so soft and deep a green that
it could pass for the pelt of some great mythical beast
whose only job is to protect frightened children
who cuddle up to it.

What a spring this is!
No hearts can be permanently broken
in all this life,
no souls dead.

How could they be
in the face of this much resurrection,
with so much pollen drifting
and the mountain laurel buds fattening
and their new leaves singing green?

Spoken into Being

Ten years since I've written
much of anything,
even a shopping list.

"You've got to stop writing that stuff,"
Mama cried, after my last book,
again and again.

I didn't mean to be proclaiming truth
for everyone and for all times.
I was telling tales as I had heard them told,
stories I loved, honoring the beloved dead,
beloved by virtue of those stories,
told and told again.

I hurt people though.
I never meant to hurt
and it hurt me too.

And so I stopped. My fingers
wouldn't write.
In my head no words formed.
My heart couldn't breathe.
I don't believe I chose it.
(But maybe I did.
The heart is a devious thing.)

Now, ten years later,
my fingers work again.
I wake up at night,

my head full of phrases
all sweet as honey in the mouth,
and in the stomach too.

My feet and hands rejoice.
This is a gift of grace,
all grace,
and with it,
all gratitude.

Now Go On Home

Now go on home,
you say to me.
You've got to get back to your life.

I am bewildered,
feeling pushed away.

No, says Mama,
I am fine now,
and so are you.

I loved you being here,
I'll always love you,
but you've got to get back.

But Mama, how am I going to do it?

Just want it badly enough.
That will do it, you say.

But here's the trick:
What do I do to want it? I ask.

Looking Around

Having swum for days
in a cold ocean with no landmarks
except the other swimmers who cannot see me,
but who go as I go,
I am so very tired.
Arms and legs hurt,
chest hurts.
Where could I be now,
I wonder, *after all this time?*

I lift my head to gasp for air and look around,
expecting nothing but more of the same—
waves, water, a bit of sky,
dark greens and blues, wet without bottom.

Though I have no idea of the time of day,
much less the date of the day itself,
I am horribly oriented.
The salty water is bitter on my lips.
My clothes weigh me down.
I hope the air will hold me
as the water does,
but I surely won't trust it.

I lift my head to look and my body shifts
and my legs hang down.
Unexpectedly, my feet touch sand,
and soft sand too.
I am nearly ashore.

Before me is a woods,
full of hemlocks with their newest needles,
light green for spring,
glowing against the darker branches.
They are soft like feathers and tall.

And there are cedar trees, sleek of limb,
symmetrical and solid,
and pines,
and maples, some red, some not,
and oaks,
and sweet gums,
and tulip poplars, the blooms just now gone.
Saplings everywhere.

There are also wild azaleas, orange as orange rind,
and pink ones too, like pale watermelon,
and blooming mountain laurel,
with the flowers' little white corners and faint red trim.
Rhododendrons bloom in every color,
pale pink to shouting magenta against their shiny leaves.

In the sun, there are daisies white and yellow,
a bit of late thrift,
something yellow that looks like goldenrod
but can't be, yet,
and the ethereal lavender blue of cornflowers.
Irises, ferns of every kind,
mosses dark and light,
thick and sparse,
grasses green and brown
where they have already gone to seed.

Birds, hummingbirds,
wood thrushes,
robins, cardinals straight from the Vatican,
woodpeckers big and little,
all with a bit of red somewhere
on their upright bodies,
bluebirds fresh from the fields,
hawks and owls.

Then, there are chipmunks,
squirrels, voles, woodchucks,
deer, foxes (beautiful, beautiful),
snakes, fish in a pond,
frogs, earthworms.

And in the middle of all this wonder
stands a green house I know,
with a porch in front,
a little white dog at the window.

A man comes out,
not a big man, but beautiful.
His hands are kind
and his mouth smiles with gentleness.
His eyes are green but not like the sea.
His beard is mostly gray
as is his curly hair.
He walks toward me slowly
so as not to frighten me.

He is holding a blue towel.
He throws it around me
as he says,
This is your house,
your dog,
your woods,
and I am your husband
who loves you.
Do you remember me?

I do.
I look at him,
then over my shoulder
at the water I've just left.
I love him.
I am afraid.

Do I have to go back? I ask.
My whole body is pickled
and swollen and my throat hurts.

Not unless you believe you must,
he answers.
But if you do,
your home will still be here
in this magical place
which is the world,
and I will be waiting for you.

I sigh with relief and still some fear.
I want to be home, I say.

I follow him through the door
and the dog comes,
leaping and prancing
and smiling, welcoming me
with his warm tongue.
We laugh
and we hold each other tight.

Weaving

*I*wouldn't go so far as to say that I am obsessed with weaving, but weaving plays a significant role in my life. Among other things, it generally keeps me sane or at least moves me in that direction when I feel stressed or helpless. Handling the beautiful yarn, soaking up the colors (especially the intense ones) and the light reflected off them, seeing a complex pattern emerge where previously I saw a mass of beautiful string, using my brain—not to mention my whole body. Weaving is good for my soul.

I haven't always woven. In fact, I didn't begin any work with fiber until later in life. I began with knitting. Two or three years before I retired, my friend Karen got me started knitting at a weekend-long faculty meeting. (Knitting is great for meetings because I can concentrate on what I am hearing while keeping my restlessness and my straying mouth at bay.) I began with store-bought yarn until I encountered hand-dyed and hand-spun yarn and was entranced by it. Soon I began spinning my own yarn as well as visiting the sheep who grew the wool. One great value-added aspect of buying the unspun wool is this: you can almost always learn the name of the sheep it is from. If you are lucky, as I was, you can then meet and maybe make friends with the particular sheep your wool is from. Sheep are wonderful animals. There aren't many pleasures greater than spinning and then knitting with the wool of sheep I love.

I never got very good at knitting, since I can't read patterns, and I soon became interested in weaving in addition to spinning and knitting. I liked the idea of the complexity of it, and I really liked the fact that if I learned something new every day for the rest of my life, I would never get to the end of what I could learn. Weaving, after all, is one of the oldest, most widespread human arts you can find. Furthermore, though it hasn't always been the case everywhere, it has generally been a woman's art. I had spent my professional life using my brain pretty exclusively for research, writing books, and teaching, and I wanted to select a craft that would involve my whole self, including my body.

I began on the floor loom by taking a class, and I can't claim that experience as a happy one. I seemed to take much longer to know what I was doing than anybody else, and there were many things I never understood at all. I often felt humiliated and embarrassed by my slowness—not by anybody there, just by myself. I knew when I got home, I wouldn't remember how to get the warp on the loom so that I could weave. (The warp comprises the up and down threads you weave into side by side.) After at least twenty tries, I called my teacher to relay my plight. "Oh, that's all right," she said, "some people take up to three times to learn to do it!" I chose not to tell her the horrible truth. I finally got the hang of it, however.

I may never be a very good weaver, but for the most part I am a happy one. Color comes easily to me, as does texture. But the complexities of weaving are opaque to me past a rather close-up point. Wrestling with my limitations while I do what I love has been a good spiritual discipline. It really is not true that "unless you do something right, it is better not to do it at all." Weaving is good for me. When I am anxious, it soothes; when I am confused or chaotic, it brings order and structure. I am able to weave beautiful, if imperfect, things that make me happy. Furthermore, the reminder of God as the Weaver of Love whom all human weavers imitate serves as a providential reminder.

When Mama died, I suddenly discovered that I couldn't weave; I couldn't stand anything about it. Before I was called to Louisville I had a great green warp on the loom to make towels as a present for her birthday. When I returned after her funeral, not only did I hate the sight of it, but at least thirty threads had snapped and were hanging off the loom in various places. This kind of spontaneous breaking had never happened to me before. It was almost spooky.

It felt like the loom itself was grieving. For a while, nothing held the same meaning it had before, and nothing acted like it used to act. Where there was comfort, there was no longer comfort. What was interesting and exciting became boring or exasperating. Even chocolate tasted bitter. What was a pleasure became a painful task. Along with my loss, it seemed that every part of my life had been thrown up in the air only to come down again in an unrecognizable pattern. Over time, this disorientation began to right itself. I enjoy my weaving again—it has been given back to me, and I am grateful.

Like me, you may feel as though you'll never live through it. I felt that way after Daddy died and when my dear aunt died too, not much later than he did. Coming home from Daddy's funeral, I'll never forget how inexplicably strange the familiar trees looked along the highway as I realized my father would never see them again in this life. How much stranger it was when mother died, more like the pain in a phantom limb, I would guess, than anything else. Ordinary life is not yet wholly back, but I not only survive; in real ways, I am thriving. The thriving feels like Mama's gift.

Today I Intended to Have a Respite

Today I intended to have a respite.
This morning, I said,
I will push clear of the dark,
and make an attempt at my ordinary life
and get to work.

So I went downstairs
where I do my weaving
(weaving is what I do, after all),
turned on the lights,
sat down on my bench,
and looked at my loom.

I didn't know what I wanted to weave,
but I had already picked out
the lovely spools of yarn
before you died
and set them out together
to weave into stripes
as fine as Joseph's coat.

Their colors were a comfort and a consolation—
roses, purples, rust, black,
maroon and lavender,
some silky, some rough but supple in my fingers,
all of them with a shine to them, at least a little bit,
all of them flesh of my flesh.

So, I got out my pattern books
to choose a design,
complex and beautiful,
delicate and subtle,
something I could put on my big loom
to weave myself away
to someplace else.

And here I faltered.
Exhaustion overtook me,
or boredom,
a loathing for
what had just pleased me.
Anyway, I couldn't concentrate,
and my chest hurt
and so did my hands.

I don't know what really happened that morning
when I think about it now.
Maybe it was a desire for respite that tripped me up
or a refusal to honor the work for its own sake
and not for my relief.
Perhaps it was a tiredness in the bone,
(God knows I'm as tired as I get).

Or it may not have been any of these at all.
Who can say?
Maybe it's as simple as this:
Maybe it's just that you can't push grief.

I Try Again

Today I try again.
Must do my work,
live in the world with everybody else.
Create what is beautiful on solid ground.

So I think about yarn,
what I've arranged downstairs
on my handmade table that I love,
made from an extra thick board, irregular in shape,
polished smooth as water.

It stands on primitive legs
with the bark still on.

I handle the yarn in my mind.
I pick up each spool,
pull a little out from the various colors,
twist them together gently,
squint at their shimmer,
judge the weight of them all together.

While I am doing this,
I am pretending to be nonchalant,
I whistle softly.
In my mind I am sneaking up
on what I intend to do.

Quickly, I decide on a pattern,
before I back out.
(It's just theoretical, I tell myself.)
It's a zigzag twill
with the zigzags going long ways,
easy to thread and easy to treadle,
right for the yarn.

Only one thing left to plan,
I tell myself.
If I were to weave it,
I would choose
the width of the cloth
and the length of it.

And here I stick:
What do I want to make?
Nothing, really, not even in my mind.
Or maybe I just don't know
what I want.

Or maybe I do.
Maybe I want my life back in a familiar form.

I want to be oriented by the compass
and the calendar,
and not by grief.

I want my Mama
alive, thirty years old,
not half my age,
and standing in the sunshine
in her sundress from the forties,
a bow on her bare shoulder and
squinting a little—

Like me, when I squint at my yarn
with my mind's eye,
not helpless and old,
but happy with everything,
absolutely everything.

Not yet, she says to me,
as I open the door to go downstairs.
Don't go down yet.
Wait a little.
I'll tell you when.

Three Days Later

"Now," Mama says.
"It's time now."

A Warp

When I got back from my second trip to mother's in March,
after the funeral when we took her apartment apart,
scattering everything,
so that her place would no longer know her again
if she were to return—
which, of course, she wouldn't,
something had happened in my own house
which had never occurred before:

I had been weaving a birthday present for Mama
for her ninety-sixth birthday,
which was coming very soon,
little hand towels in a vivid green,
the wefts a bouquet of colors,
a complex, beautiful pattern of Celtic braids.

I came home to broken warp threads on my loom
(remember that the warp provides the frame into which
the other threads are woven
to make the cloth).

The yarn had been strong and gleaming,
smooth and threaded just right on the loom
before I left.
I had woven two or three pieces of cloth already
before I was called to Mama's for her last days.
The towels had been coming out just right,
and I left them without a thought.
What is weaving, anyway, in the great unweaving of death?

When everything was over, however,
and I came home,
and I could bring myself to walk downstairs again
to greet my loom,
something utterly unexpected had happened:

several warp threads had broken,
snapped in the silence of no work,
now hanging limp,
breath gone out of the yarn,
I suppose, with nothing left to sustain it.

I abandoned the project,
turned around, and went back upstairs,
unable even to consider what to do with it.
I could have repaired it, I suppose,
but I had no heart for it,
no breath of my own
to bring it back to life.
Ultimately, I ripped what was left of it
off the loom and threw it out,
a great waste and a greater relief.

I am weaving again for myself now and oddly, perhaps,
for Mama too
(she is the one who summoned me back to it, after all, a few weeks
after my mercy killing of that green warp).
Today, I am weaving again—and furiously,
using lovely yarns of every color,
every size and texture
including grief—
using words, feathers,
sounds and smells,
transparent light and heavy darkness,
none of this visible,
but weaving for the first time fearlessly
with seriousness and joy
with intelligence and delight.

Good Day, Bad Day

I woke this morning,
miracle of miracles,
rested.
All night long it rained hard
and thundered softly.
A great combination for the usually sleepless.

The dog cuddled beside me till after nine
(and wouldn't go out),
the coffee was tasty,
toast burnt like I like it,
and the paper full of easy articles to read.

A good day to try again to weave! I said.
So I finished my breakfast,
had a shower,
and decorated myself in clean clothes.
I got out a pad of paper,
planned out the colors for the warp,
selected the yarn,
determined where the stripes would go
and how wide each would be,
measured for the warp
(black bamboo and variegated dark pink rayon).
Though I still did not settle on a pattern,
I went downstairs to prepare the warp.

Now, Mama, you need to know that
when you make a warp
(the long-ways yarn you will put on the loom
to later weave the weft into),
you start by winding the warp
on pegs on the wall,
counting the threads as you go,
to measure it and keep it straight and even.

It sounds easy, and it is.
The trick is, your mind can't wander.
You have to pay attention.
Today, once more, it was no use.

I started out well enough with the winding,
alternating beautiful bands of black and color,
but in the end, I couldn't do it.
In spite of my care,
my clumsy fingers tangled the pink irrevocably
and unwittingly, pulling too hard
on the fragile yarn,
I broke the black three times
and had to throw a lot away.
I never did get it right.

I haven't given up, mind you,
but I've quit for the day.
I sigh and sigh.
The rain continues,
clattering on the roof
and going through the gullies like mad water.

It is getting dark and
there is no one outside.
The dog sleeps on the couch and won't get up.
I would lie down with him and sleep too,
but it's too late for that;
I've slept myself out, and besides,
I'm quivering with anxiety.

Too bad for now.
That's just the way it is with grief,
I tell myself.

A Fox Today

This morning, walking the dog
much too early, with the sun barely up,
a fox ran across our path.
It was quite close,
an amazing bright rust,
nose pointed straight ahead,
tail, thick and soft,
straight out behind.

It was altogether beautiful, that fox,
breathtaking, really,
graceful and shapely,
low to the ground
with pointed ears and a pointed nose
and tiny, very fast feet.

Then I came home and finished my first weaving project
since Mama died—I've been too clumsy, too sad,
too heavy-handed and distracted before,
the very opposite of that focused, glowing fox.

The project took all day, and it turned out well.
Black bamboo, variegated pink, grey, and purple rayon,
stripes delicate and distinct,
a scarf that should please anyone.
And, as part of the finishing is always
washing what was just woven,
it's drying in the bathroom shower now.

But in the meantime,
with all this going on,
I am having a sinking spell,
as the old folks would say.
I am tired and my eyes hurt.

Fox or no,
weaving or no,
now I want clean sheets
and a soft bed.
I want my Mama.

Life Is Coming Back

Life is coming back now.
It comes in bits and pieces,
then, in big chunks,
dropped on the floor
and making much noise.

For the last three days,
I have been weaving something beautiful,
a scarf, but really just an excuse to make cloth.
It is bamboo and rayon of different thicknesses
and variegated rayon too.
The black bamboo in the stripes
is thin and crinkly;
not like what pandas eat
but tasty, nonetheless.

The pink rayon is shiny and flat in the warp
before it's woven in diamonds up the sides.
Lovely by itself—
indeed, I've been saving it for something special—
it turns thin and a bit dull
combined as it is with black weft
in its place in the cloth.

Making more subtle diamonds,
the variegated rayon
of deep pink and lavender and gray,
alone looks like it did in the beginning.

Occupying the middle space,
it is thick,
deep, mysterious, and opulent,
and textured too,
with hills and valleys between the black and pink.

Two parts, then, one of colors and textures,
one of pattern laying over it all,
or really, woven through it inseparably.
It is beautiful and it pleases me.

Green is everywhere I look outside,
the warp and weft of spring,
a hackneyed metaphor,
except there is no way
what I am looking at is hackneyed.

It is life coming back,
my life,
simple, complex patterns
becoming visible,
lovely in what is given,
beloved, even,
but not so noisy now.
Utterly silent, in fact,
and sweet as my weaving,
sweet as spring.

It Is the Oddest Thing

Almost the last time I saw Mama, she said to me,
"You know, you could weave bookmarks
for Christmas presents.
Everybody would love them."

I didn't answer.
I didn't think anyone would love them,
and, moreover, I would have to use yarn so thin
I could hardly handle it.

Remembering this conversation now,
I can barely breathe.
Mama was so close to death
she could have fallen over into it
in a skinny minute,
yet she noticed something
as everyday as Christmas,
made an ordinary suggestion,
about as bound to a mortal life as it could be.

How can I begin to say it?
Mama was already out of time,
living mostly somewhere else,
but she was here too,
as solid as the ground under my feet.
And if I had paid attention
I could tell you the exact hour and minute
on the clock
this woman spoke.

Two things to say about this.
First, I know this is the way we all live,
here in time and also beyond time, all at once,
dead in one world or the other
and also alive.

The other thing I am not sure I can find words for:
Hearing mother's voice now in my head
I am drawn back into such an immediate intimacy with her
that I could tell you the time to the second.
Here we both are in her little living room
full of the sight and smell of her,
she in her pretty bathrobe Linda gave her,
me in my old nightgown.
I feel in my hands the Blue Willow cup she loves,
full of coffee, hot and sloshing over the sides a little.
I bring it to her and look around for the morning paper.
Toast is in the toaster, plate ready for it along with jelly.
My breath is in my ears.
I've slept on the couch and my neck is stiff,
and I wonder what I will eat for breakfast.

"You know, you could weave bookmarks," she says,
and she is here, or rather, I am there with her, really there
in the closest circle of her touch.
How can this be?

And so I ponder but can't get a grip on it
however hard I try.

Time is surely beyond the grasp of my imagining
and so is reality; God, neither here nor there
and yet, everywhere at once.

It strikes me again and again:
What a strange place to which my mother has gone—
intimate as breath, more distant than the galaxies.
Such a very odd place is the communion of the saints
toward which we all are moving.

A New Weave Structure

I am learning a new weave structure.
It is called double weave.
I've wanted to learn it for a long, long time
but up until now, it has been too hard for me.

Its characteristics are these:
If you warp your loom carefully
with twice as many pieces of yarn
(we call them ends) as usual,
you can weave two layers of cloth at the same time,
two wefts, one above the other,
completely separate from each other.
It is astounding,
almost a miracle, seemingly impossible,
only, it most certainly is possible.

Then, as if that were not enough,
you can weave it in such a way
that you connect the two layers along one edge
so that when you take the whole thing off the loom,
you have one single piece of cloth folded up the center—
good for tablecloths or blankets or other things you might fancy.

You can make tubes this way too,
woven up each side but hollow in the middle.
Furthermore, you can stitch the whole thing together,
with the loom, making it like a quilt with a pattern,
weaving it into just about anything that you desire,
but with the two parts no longer separable.

All of this double weave makes me think of Mama—
no, it makes me long for Mama.
I weave the top layer of my own life
while Mama weaves below me,
stitch for stitch, me, a red layer.

Hers is a layer of grief,
these two separable from each other in theory,
but in truth, joined at the edges,
stitched together throughout the body.

It is the quilted stitches that make the pattern
in double weave,
and it is done in this way:
By a skillful manipulation of the loom
threads from the bottom layer are pulled through to the top,
two colors on one side,
the opposite two on the other,
the pattern reversed.

This cloth is beautiful and very sturdy
for all its intricacies,
red on the top,
and coming through from the bottom,
the designs and threads of grief.
It is as strong as it can be,
stronger than bone or rock,
more powerful than eagles,
more powerful than a great waterfall.

In fact, I sometimes am afraid when I think of it.
What if the cloth I'm woven into with Mama
is too strong altogether?
What if it is stronger even than death itself?

Wild Things

I have always been drawn to the beauty of wild things or at least of nonhuman things that seemed to me to have mysterious lives of their own. As a child, I was fascinated by a beautiful mound of healthy kelly-green, furry moss. When things got tough for me in the human world, I would imagine that I was as tiny as an ant who lived in the moss, sheltered by the leaves of tall weeds like trees. I sat on boulders made of miniscule bits of gravel or slept on the soft ground, safely hidden under fallen leaves. Throughout childhood the thought of green, soft moss could comfort me when I most needed it.

It wasn't only moss that brought me ease of heart as a child. I could also be soothed by the red color of a single oak leaf in the fall or an oddly veined rock I found in the grass. Discovering a tiny hidden flower under a bush or the top of an acorn or even a little piece of quartz crystal could bring me a flash of happiness different from anything else. It seems to me now that small living things, squirrels, for example, drew me closest to them. I suspected they had incomprehensible lives of their own that I could almost imagine living in myself, alternative worlds into which I could almost see.

This state of understanding changed a little as I grew older, but much of it didn't. I see more now when I pay attention, which I often do not, and I am more overwhelmed by beauty that I now realize has nothing to do with me at all—except as it brings me half-understood messages of God's goodness and love. Two sights from my adult past I remember now. The first is a huge oak tree outside my floor-to-ceiling window before my daughter was born. It was covered with dark red leaves of such an intensity that their red color and shapes reflected off the white walls of the apartment where I lived. It was truly astonishing and it hardly seemed possible, but there it was. Through that tree I received an obscure message of hope and beauty at a place in my life that seemed so hopeless I was not sure I could survive it.

The second sight was my first encounter with moon jellyfish in a small tank in a large aquarium. I had never seen anything like them before: They were perfectly white and undulating up and down in the dim water like wet linen handkerchiefs. No eyes or mouths were visible, only a star-shaped pattern in their middle, which was denser than the edge. They were graceful beyond belief and at the same time as alien to me as living creatures can get. They struck me speechless, and I focused on them to the point of immobility. Their beauty and the secret world they carried me into mesmerized me. Once again, I was at a place in my life where I desperately needed help. What I saw, how God spoke to me, the message I was given that day, is still beyond my powers to explain past this point. But it was so good, so vivid, and so healing that I suspect it will come back to me as I die.

In my grief over my mother's death, I found myself in a state of heightened awareness for many months every time I went out the front door to walk my dog. Almost daily it was like living again through the experience of the moon jellies, only now everything had this mesmerizing quality—leaves, rocks, clouds, flowers, yes, and moss, mushrooms, branches, colors, textures, smells, everything. And like those jellyfish long ago, all that I saw spoke messages to me of goodness, gratitude, hope, longing, love, and occasionally fear. None of it served to remind me of what I already knew. The encounter was with reality itself, which reflects God, at a deeper level than I customarily meet it.

This sharpening of the senses in wonder over the natural world around me lasted for several months and then gradually faded. Now it is gone, perhaps because my need for it is no longer so strong as it was, perhaps because the sharpness of my grief is dulled a little. I still see with my eyes what I saw a few months ago, but it is no longer the same. I miss it.

Even now I frequently am given back a bit of that gift for a little while as I observe the coming of winter. The thought of winter draws me in this special way, as a tiny part of what may be its meaning fills my heart. More than ever, even without this temporary heightened awareness of the physical world, I am comforted by the everyday things around me, all things wild and beautiful and beyond understanding. I affirm that they are very good, which does not surprise me. After all, everything that is, from the smallest particle to the largest galaxy, reflects God to us if we pay attention.

Wisteria

All over the mountains wisteria blooms.
It hangs down in great swaths
from every half-dead tree.
It drapes itself on telephone poles
and falling-down barns.
It throws itself mightily
where the kudzu will shortly come,
hoping to defeat its enemy's empire in advance.
Its scent is everywhere,
inescapable as wet earth,
heavy and heavier still.

This year, against every expectation,
the wisteria behind our house
is not yet blooming.
Only small green curled-up things
embellish our dry vines
and tiny crumpled handkerchiefs
of purple, not fit for more
than a house finch's sneezes.

Whatever the wisteria should choose to do,
it is another matter with
the bleeding hearts under the front window.

Not so much as a stem above ground
a week ago before we left
to take apart all Mama's things,
we have come back to find them up
and blooming their hearts out,
white and red,
beautiful and bleeding everywhere.

A Cold Rain Today

A cold rain today.
Forty-one degrees.
Blossoms are knocked off the trees,
poor things.
Daffodils beaten flat,
their leaves splayed and shivering.
Even the violets are curled up and hunched down.
(Except for the thrift, of course.
You can't beat down thrift.)

But the roots ignore the flowers,
however they feel
they soak up water
then soak up more.
You can almost hear them slurping.

Black roots, deep and shallow,
hold the earth together. They send up green,
flowers everywhere, fruit,
every green thing that grows upon the earth.

Mama, I feel you
deep in the earth, celebrating the rain,
sending down deep roots,
sprouting green.
I feel my own buds coming
with the spring,
with you,
also to celebrate the rain.

Violets, Thrift

There is a patch of violets
blooming by the side of the road
after the railroad track,
the big purple kind
and the white kind too,
with darker purple veins,
the first ones of the year.

Oh, yes, and there is
a patch of bright pink thrift
in the grass by the bridge,
quite a lot of it.
"Now save your money,"
Mama used to say.
That's what the thrift reminds me of.

More Flowers

While this spring the leaves continue
a light green that multiplies itself continually
from tree to tree
and shrub to shrub,
the flowers are changing.

Today I saw a wild rose bush
blooming in the rain,
the branches cascading down
like the rain itself,
flowers from the crown of its head
to the wet earth below it.
The flowers were small, close together and pink,
not white as I would expect,
but so extravagant!

It was off the road at the edge of a field,
and something about how it sat
made me think there had once been a house there,
now long gone.
(It happens like this in the country.)

This got me thinking.
Maybe that bush was not a wild rose at all.
Perhaps it was once a tame plant,
growing by the side of a porch where
a woman shelled peas and washed clothes
and smelled its blossoms,
and children played.

Something would have happened
to make the rose go so very feral.
Someone would have died or abandoned the house,
with its plants around it.
Or it may simply have fallen in on itself,
still occupied.
(This also happens in the country.)

It was a solitary bush.
A feral bush,
a bush somehow orphaned,
and rained on,
and left by itself, alone,
in an unplanted field.

Out on the Highway

It's still spring, but now we are in the middle of it.
The grass has been mown for the first time
along the road, and
the little flowers are going fast.

It's most certainly still spring though.
The leaves on the trees
are the colors that puppies would be
if they were green.
They act like them too,
blowing and tossing every which way,
while the evergreens,
the hemlocks and cedars and pines,
in their darker green,
watch over them
to protect them against predators and
to keep them out of trouble.

Gum Trees

All summer when we go out,
my little dog and I,
for the first walk of our day,
the stars are waiting—
I don't mean the stars that are in the sky,
shining beautiful and far off in the darkness on a clear night
without much moon.
I'm thinking of the morning stars of the sweet gum trees,
stars made up of fingers spread out from each palm of each leaf,
straight sided and narrow,
and perfect beyond words.
They are the hands of angels, I believe,
visible to me
and to my dog too
only by their hands,
faces, wings and bodies hidden, rustling,
somewhere in their trees
otherwise invisible in green.
Surely they are the hands of stars
made ordinary, everyday, and green among us,
mysterious, inexplicable, nevertheless.
They shine at me in the early mornings
on their stiff red stems as trustworthy as any host.
Still, I never can quite trust that those fingers haven't curled closed
into the palms and left me
without stars,
without angels while I've slept.
It may be different now.
Last week I went away to Alabama
to a beautiful place
with happy work
and good friends.
I was just where I wanted to be,

but I missed my home,
the mountains where I live,
my husband, my little white dog
and our walks, and the trees, most specifically,
the star and angel trees,
mysterious in the woods.
It would not be too much to say
I suffered for them or at least, restlessly, longed for them.
But Saturday, the day before I left,
I sat in a rocking chair on the wide porch in Alabama,
looking out on the lawn between our buildings,
and there they were.
In a good-sized tree,
with a long trunk and perfectly symmetrical body,
there were the stars,
the angels' hands
I thought I'd left at home.
How they got there, I do not know,
but they comforted my heart,
those green leaves,
as they rustled, "Trust.
God will not abandon you in the universe.
We are here now,
and next year we will be too.
Angels are not lost
(except that one)
and neither are the stars who are our hands.
Though the mountains fall into the sea,
always, we are here."

And so I learned again,
while grief sharpens my vision to let me see,
sometimes it lies.
God will not leave us comfortless,
God will not leave us without joy.

Tulip Poplars

Mama loved tulip poplar blossoms.
I remember the look on her face
when she picked one up once
in our backyard and wondered at its delicacy,
and its long fall from a tall tree.

Two days ago, walking
outside our mountain house,
I came upon a tulip poplar blossom in the road.
It had been crushed by a car,
but I still recognized its soft green
and softer orange.
They really do look like nothing else.

I couldn't find where it had come from,
some high tree, perhaps
(they do grow so very fast)
or a sapling so small as to be invisible.
Wherever its home was,
it was nowhere in sight.

Today, however, I found it,
not just the elusive tree that was the source of that blossom
but the very way those flowers grow upon the tree.
Do you know,
they come out at the end of a branch
exactly where an awkward fan
of many stems and new leaves are already growing.
Behind the flowers, dark green foliage.
In front of them, the tangled nearly translucent
        light green of spring.

The sight was odd enough
that I had to look two or three times
before I could make sense of what I was seeing.
And even so, I may not have it exactly right.

There was a secret in this tree,
or at least a metaphor
I could almost grasp.
But really, I would prefer not to explain it.

Wisps of Ferns

Wisps of ferns
pale green
soft as feathers.

May apples
flat as doilies on a table
but without the table.

Now there is white clover blooming
among the violets,
dogwoods,
half blossoms
half leaves.

And weeping cherries,
and apple blossoms,
the bradford pears in leaf,
red haze of maples,
stalks of Solomon's seal,
odd azaleas,
redbud—

none of these was here
on that Palm Sunday
when you died,

except for the Lenten roses
(it was Lent, after all,
and they were to be expected)
and a few daffodils.

The daffodils are gone now
and the fiddlehead ferns are tuning up.
Meanwhile, the Lenten roses bloom and bloom.

Beauty Is in the Eye of the Beholder

Beauty is in the eye of the beholder
but in God's everlasting eye as well.

Ten days ago,
I saw an amazing mountain laurel
all in bloom down a ways from us
where three roads meet.
It was a tall bush, thick and spreading,
towering almost like a tree,
though its branches came down thickly to the ground.
Astounding indeed.
Its blossoms were perfectly white
with no customary dust of pink at all.

Seeing it did not so much remind me
of brides on a sunny day:
It put me there among them
in a kind of vision.
For that time, it was only happiness
and brightness,
little mints and wedding cakes,
and fat white ribbons,
and flowers too,
perhaps the mountain laurels themselves.

That was two weeks ago.
For three days after that I saw brides
when I passed that tree,
and then we had a rain—
not a strong rain,
not enough to knock the blossoms off,
but a rain nonetheless.

And then, when the little storm was gone,
the brides and all their lovely paraphernalia
were gone too.

The bush was transformed
(transformed itself?)
into a towering white archangel
with a clear and flaming sword.
I don't mean it looked like an archangel now,
in some literal sense, you understand,
any more than it had really looked like brides before.

Nonetheless, it was an angel,
and a big one at that,
an important one too.

I couldn't say what either of these revelations meant,
or even whether they should be taken together
in the nature of early summer.
But I do know this: they stood as sentinels,
rather, when I saw them,
as one and the same sentinel
over all creation
with its beauty and fragility and fierceness too.

More days of rain have come and gone now,
and those white, perfectly geometrical flowers
that measured all the world in their shapes
have come and gone too.
They are brown and white now,
well, mostly brown,
announcing the utter end of spring,
the beginning of summer,
and the ubiquitous presence of winter
soon to come.

But then, the spring again.
The brides are already planning
and the archangel is taking fencing lessons.

All this is beautiful to me,
as it is beautiful to God

who creates it, enclosing it,
and bringing it to God's completion.
When that will be, I cannot say,
and I don't need to say either,
or how that will be.
All things belong to God
and it is very good.

Wild

Again, it rained all night.
This morning on the way to church,
everything was lush beyond belief.
Privet bushes blooming to the sky
spaced randomly among the tall ferns
and the blackberry bushes
with the new berries coming,
and the great mountain laurels white
and a little pink
interspersed among the hemlocks and cedars,
pines and maples,
sweet gums and oaks and poplars.

The high privets were in bloom
(they still are),
tangled, long-armed; at the end of those arms, fingers of blossoms
with their odd smell.
For a long time I couldn't recognize them
for what they were,
only having noticed them before in cities,
arranged as hedges,
prim and old-fashioned
as the lace-up, high-heeled teachers' shoes
of my childhood.

Here away even from a town,
the privets grow wild
and live wild too,
as far as I can tell.

But going down the road today,
across the road from the thickest,
most exuberant privets of all,
I saw a lawn around a house,
vegetation deliberately cut down
and replaced with short, smooth grass.
A good, free people had been sold into slavery.
Why would anyone choose to do it?

Two years ago, a neighbor on our road
cleaned out the land in the woods around his house.
The worst that happened,
besides the cool and lovely ferns demolished,
was his hacking down of the blooming spikes of foxgloves,
pinky purple, freckled on the inside,
excitedly awaiting the coming foxes.

"What should I plant?" The man asked my husband,
who was still unaware of the slaughter.
"You could try ferns," my husband said.
"It's just right for ferns."
"Oh, no," replied our neighbor,
"I want neat grass,
I want a lawn!"

But wild is what is wanted in the mountains,
and wild is what I want too.
Mystery, the growing things shouting,
extravagance beyond my own control,
shades of green unfettered
in places I almost can't imagine,
green things calling God.

But a lawn?
If I wanted tame, I would live in a city.
Every place I looked
there would be grass,
clipped and smoothed,
fertilized and weeded,
around houses and offices,
apartments and parking lots,
shopping centers and police stations.

The neighbor wasn't back this year.
His grass never grew.
The ferns and spiky foxgloves have returned, however,
rendering his land all wild again.
There are more foxes now than ever.

It makes me happy.
Wild is what is needed in the mountains.
Wild is what I need.
Wild is what I need,
and wild is what I have.

The Great Mystery

*D*eath is a mystery to me as I know it has always been to people throughout the ages. How can a human being who has lived a life in time, who has experienced so much, who thinks and feels and loves so specifically, who is conscious in the way we are conscious, who is flesh and blood and nervous system and bone, be here on earth one minute and then, the next, simply gone from it? How can anybody go from something to nothing all at once? Whatever the scientific explanation, it doesn't make sense to my heart. It seems impossible. Yet this is our life experience on earth.

For that matter, birth itself offers the same kind of mystery as death. Coming into human existence doesn't happen so suddenly as death, but it happens just the same. Last year there was no child in that family down the road; one year later, a baby with a name is part of the same family, a baby already with a mind of her own who responds to her parents, to food, and to much of the world around her. A hundred years ago my mother did not exist. Then she did exist, and now once again she doesn't. If this isn't a mystery, ordinary as it looks, nothing is.

Consider our individual human lives. None of us knows the depths of our own being, said an early Christian writer when speaking of the Lord's Prayer. It is only known to God. We human beings are mysteries of God, from whom we come. This means that however much we are convinced that we truly know another person through and through, we don't because we can't. How wonderful to know absolutely that other people are not simply extensions of ourselves, that they have lives utterly unknown to us! If nothing else, the knowledge of it assures us that we are not alone in the universe; but rather, we are surrounded by a large cloud of witnesses through time and space, including our beloved dead, as well as the unknown dead.

And God is the greatest and best mystery of all, for all of reality springs from God, was created by God, is held safe in God, and will be completed in God. Julian of Norwich affirms that all things are in God and God is in all things. There is no place not filled with God, nor any person either, and we have done nothing to make this happen. We live in a universe of God's grace whether we know it or not and whether we want it or not.

Everything that is, including we ourselves, is held forever in God's love, in God's grace and mystery. Mama is in it, as am I. Grief is real and also held in God's mystery. Yet love is the greatest mystery in our amazing universe. It is given to us as a way to participate in life. It is the root and cause and completion of all things in God. It means we can trust that all whom we love will ultimately be given back to us—Mama included—in a way we cannot know. But why do we need to know how that will be? God's love is everything. God's love, like our own smaller loves, is the Great Mystery that holds all other mysteries whole and safe, and it is wondrously good.

Crows

Going into town to meet my friends
for our regular Tuesday night dinner
at the Mexican place we love,
there were crows along the highway—
not one or two crows
as I might have expected, but scores of them.

None of them was working,
as far as I could tell,
pecking out eyes of roadkill
or screaming at their neighbors
or looking for a tasty piece of trash
or maybe robbing nests.

They weren't in flocks either.

Rather, I saw as I drove past,
each solitary crow was walking slowly,
strutting in the short green grass,
each body held upright on strong legs,
each back as flat as a bird's back can be,
each head held right above the shoulders,
wings tucked in just so.

And feathers! Real plumage adorned those crows,
tail feathers stiff and smooth,
shiny black and clean;
they were as sleek as anything.
And so full of themselves!
Their slow walk was practiced,
fit, they believed, for the coronation of a queen.

But of course, all I've said is fanciful.
What those black birds were really doing in the grass
I couldn't say,

and I wouldn't want to say even if I could.
No matter what we want to think,
the lives of crows are hidden from us,
as are all the lives in our most wondrous world,
as even our own lives are,
most blessedly.

Across the Road

There is a hemlock across the road,
not large but not small either.
This morning, coming home with my little white dog,
I noticed it.
There was a little twig
toward the bottom that was moving fast,
turning with what had to be the wind,
only there was no wind.

It is an odd hemlock,
low and misshapen by the woods,
pressed down upon by many other trees.

It is frightening in its way.
The bottom third of it is growing exuberantly,
extravagantly even,
long, light-green fingers at the end of each dark branch.

At the same time, amidst all this growing,
every branch is covered with patches
of what appears to be dirty lichen.
They are the leftovers from the former visitation
of the hoards of tiny monsters
who cover the hemlock with their white eggs
to kill the tree.

And, sure enough,
the top two-thirds of the hemlock
is dying.
Though nothing has fallen off,
large chunks of it have turned
the golden brown of a corpse tree.
Death will be soon.
Who knows if it is suffering.

Meanwhile, however, the bottom is growing,
impossible as it would seem.
Perhaps it is not so much exuberantly as I had thought,
as it is in desperation,
a panic for its life.

Pondering everything,
I ask this question now
for my friend the tree:
Can an evergreen still be ever green
even after it has died?

Those Hemlocks

Those hemlocks, the most dignified
and stately of trees,
are bemusing me in this late spring.
The fact is,
at the end of each branch
those new needles are so bright
against the older darker green foliage,
chicken feet have developed.
Long toes, sometimes two
and sometimes three,
have appeared where the new growth is,
longer than is seemly,

some with little nails on the tips,
all awkward once you notice them.
You pretend you don't.
You can't help but laugh at such dignity
dressed in a chicken suit!

I don't understand how they are coming on,
but I dare not judge.
I, after all, have crow's feet on my face,
and what's the difference?
Whatever the species,
bird's feet are bird's feet.
I imagine they are no more becoming
to me than they are to the hemlocks.

Still, we have to have those feet, I'm afraid, to grow.
Both are a sign of perpetually renewing youth,
manifesting themselves on our older bodies
incongruously, at least in appearance,
birth where you don't expect it
on human beings,
something else close to it
on the hemlocks.

Mortality hurts.
We all die,
we all suffer,
and it comes on little by little
as long as we live.
Continual birth is a consolation for it,
at least from the human perspective.
I don't know how hemlocks feel about their chicken feet.
I've never asked them,
and I don't propose to now.

Silver

This morning, much too early,
walking down the stone path
from the back door of our church
to my car in the parking lot,
dozing on my feet,
muddle-headed and too sleepy to see much around me,
I was given a revelation of beauty
so clear, so sharp,
that all at once my whole self was
taken up in delight.

When this revelation came to me
the sun was well up but not high.
The sky was bright.
The light was even and happy,
as I was too, even muddled.
Flowers, tall and golden,
red and purple,
leafed with every kind of green
had been planted at the entrance to the path
as it flowed out of the parking lot
toward our church.
The flowers were living their own lives,
not interested in any of ours.

I had been to the early service
and, still stumbly,
walking between them,
I was looking down.
I didn't want to fall.

Then, all at once, this is what came to me:
Strands of silver no thicker than a sewing thread
were making gleaming patterns

on the rocks I walked upon.
I could not tell if they were beads or linked chains,
but I'll tell you this:
Thin as a hair, the light shone through them
as well as on them
and reflected back to me blindingly,
like sun on a mirror,
like sun on glass or ice.

Surprised, I stepped back and they disappeared.
I stepped forward and there they were again,
flashing glory everywhere.

They were the tracks of snails
or, even worse, of hated slugs
(nothing is so ugly as a slug).

And so in that moment,
ordinary and plain,
I was shown again in flashes of silver
what we all know and I always forget.
In all things,
in every being,
in everything created,
in the ugliest of creatures,
even in us at our worst,
there is God walking,
pacing out great looping paths of beauty,
thin as anything.
Mostly they are invisible unless the light is right
and we are watching.
They invite us to see them,
calling out to us very quietly,
"Look, look!"

Gold

This is the time of year we live with gold.
The field near our house is full of it—
tall spikes of goldenrod,
yellow and furry like the throats of spring irises
but much bigger,
and black-eyed susans on delicate branching plants
like wild sunflowers.
Gold is everywhere,
wiping out the memory of the pink of rose bushes
in a field,
and white daisies and Queen Anne's lace
(except the Queen Anne's lace
has left behind its blossoms
that have turned into great upside-down spiders,
dead as they can be,
dried up and dreadful).

Of course, not everything that blooms now is gold.
There is the long-awaited ironweed,
with its clustered blossoms a deep red purple,
suitable for a Byzantine emperor
and holding its own against
the color of the gold.

But there are two more plants
with nothing rich about them
that don't fit at all.

First, there is Joe Pye weed.
Unlike the goldenrod, it grows in solitary spikes, by itself,
mostly one flower per plant, if you can think
of a whole cluster of little blooms as a single flower
the size of a large and lacy cabbage head
swaying on top of a long stalk.

The texture is wrong for the season,
and so is the color:
A dusty lavender with a whole lot of tan to it
that finally fades to brown.
It is as out of place as a woman in a fancy, frilly dress
standing chatting in a gas station as though
she thinks she belongs there.

The other is the thistle.
All summer long I have watched them
send their prickly selves up and up.
I've never seen them so high.
Now as tall as a tall and skinny basketball player,
they loom over the fields and roadsides,
leaves drying up on the stems
curly, sticking close to the stalks,
as ugly as anything beside the extravagant richness
of the goldenrods.

But their blossoms!
At the very top of each high thistle is a flower,
the color, a pale and shining lavender,
absolutely pure as babies' skin,
without blemish, without wound,
single puffs, soft amongst the prickles
that would rip your hands to shreds,
single small puffs of clear light
so very beautiful
you can hardly look away.

Beauty comes in such unexpected places,
seasons and situations
so incongruous it might seem imaginary.
But beauty is never imaginary.
It is always real, if so in flowers,
just as much in us.

A Day for a Picnic

Once out of bed for the day,
I walk to the bathroom and look in the mirror.
Every morning what I see is more or less the same,
hair, two eyes looking at me,
nose, two ears, one on each side,
a mouth, sometimes smiling,
sometimes not,
a chin.
There are lines and puffy parts,
dark and light.
Mostly I look older,
but I go through younger times too.
I don't spend much time.
It's all familiar,
and I'm not sure how much of me
I'm looking at anyway.

Thirty years ago in spring we went on a picnic,
our family did,
beside a sandy-bottomed lake.
The day was warm and sunny,
and there was a breeze that, among other work,
carried the sweet smells of new leaves,
the mysterious scents of fish nesting in the water,
and charcoal fires readying themselves
for the lunches of the children.
It was a lovely day, given to daydreaming,
a good time to go out fishing.

As for me, I sat by the shore
in a folding chair to doze and contemplate the sunlight
reflected on the face of the water.

Nodding, I did this a long while,
until my eyes were drawn without realizing it
across the calm of the lake
back toward shore.

And then, a small miracle.
Suddenly, acutely attentive now,
I found myself no longer
looking at the surface of the water
but right through it
to the yellow sandy bottom
upon which there was a gleaming pattern—
clear black lines,
outlining small geometrical shapes,
each perfect,
each golden,
and each slowly shifting form continuously.

I could hardly breathe or turn my head.
In fact, for a few minutes, I suppose,
I could not move at all.
What wonder was I seeing?
I asked myself.

I knew it was a mystery,
being written out for me
in a language I either didn't know
or I knew so well I couldn't make out the words,
but let there be no mistake:
My heart was nearly stopped
as I encountered God.
I was addressed by name
and spoken to.

I sat there, watching, listening, for a long time,
almost able to read that alien, bottom script,
but not quite, as the mysterious lines shifted,
and I tried to study where they came from.

Then, at last I saw what made the letters:
It was the sunlight,
falling on the crests of tiny waves,
as the water washed in toward me to the shore.
They hardly had crests, those small ripples,
but nonetheless, each black line on the golden bottom
was, somehow, a shadow cast
by a combination of moving surface and the sun.

What I saw that day was not an optical illusion,
though it might have been,
and not a fancy either.
I believe that day I was given a glimpse, a glance, rather,
into reality itself
as it flows from God
and complicates itself
and transmutes itself through light
and the matter of all things, ever shifting,
ever shining,
ever deeper in one dimension through another,
through all of time,
and black holes and stars,
through black lines and gold
beyond following.

But it doesn't matter.
There is no need to understand anything but this:
The surfaces of all things reflect the light.
The depths of all things mirror back God,
and it is all beautiful beyond belief,
mysterious, trustworthy, unknowable,
but true, all perfectly true,
and all of it is very good.

Remembering

I am sitting on the porch here in the mountains
and remembering, if that is the word for it.
It is the end of spring, early summer,
two months since Mama died.

The sounds and the smells of the season
are overwhelming.
Woodpeckers drumming like ghostly jackhammers,
the whip-poor-wills in the early dawn.

There was a little bird close to the house
last night suddenly singing
in the sweet spring air
so close, so excruciatingly beautiful
that it hurt me to hear it.
I didn't know what kind of bird it was,
something brown and nearly invisible,
I would guess.

But in the otherwise silence of the night,
in the moonless darkness,
it suddenly seemed to me to be trapped in our chimney,
a small bird filling the space between the stars
with its innocent proclamation
of the goodness of all things
in the place of its suffering to come it hadn't yet recognized.
I didn't think I could bear to hear its dying,
its pitiful flapping against chimney wall.
It was too painful to imagine,
nevertheless, I couldn't help myself.

All that I see celebrates creation
with that little bird,
the fox across the road,
these snakes and lizards,

each dark leaf, each tiny flower,
the perfectly symmetrical mountain laurels,
the orange fish in the pond,
the white daisies and the yellow blooms beside them
(they are far enough away in the fields
that no one except God will ever see their faces),
my dog, my hands and feet,
my own heart, in spite of myself.

Do animals know they will die,
that all whom they love will also die,
or is it only we who carry the image of God?

How do we live from day to day
with so much joy, so much pain,
and so much grief?
Yet what other way is there
to live as human beings
in the immensity and tenderness of the heart of God?

As it was, last night, while I listened,
I heard
that the singer was not trapped at all.
While I was still in the grip of my yearning
over its fragility and beauty,
without a sound of wings
I heard its song receding.
With no help from me—
what could I have done for it?—
it flew away.

I stayed behind, myself,
only remembering,
remembering and wondering.

The Dates of My Writing

Mama died on March 24, 2013

March 19	Mama Who Is Dying
March 20	Writing as My Mother Dies
March 22	Two or Three Days After I Arrived
March 23	I Think I May Be Grieving
March 23	Everything about This Hurts
March 23	Gentle, Gentle
March 24	Two Days Till Your Birthday
March 26	Clothes
March 26	March 26, Your Birthday
March 27	For Her Memorial: They Were All Easter Clothes
March 28	Today We Put Your Casket in the Ground
March 28	Holy Thursday
March 29	Good Friday
March 29	Good Friday, Still
March 30	Easter Saturday
March 31	Easter
April 1	The Eighth Day
April 1	The Burden of Your Sadness
April 1	Brothers
April 2	Not Quite Liminal
April 2	Mama, I Don't Know
April 2	Violets, Thrift
April 3	News
April 3	Linda, There Are No Words
April 3	Whether Report
April 3	On the Road to Cherry Log
April 4	Shelley, Here You Come
April 4	Spoken into Being

Roberta C. Bondi graduated from Southern Methodist University in 1963 with a BA in English literature. She attended Perkins School of Theology, then went on to earn an MA in Semitic languages and a DPhil in the theology of the early church at the University of Oxford. She taught for a number of years at the University of Notre Dame before she began teaching at Candler School of Theology at Emory University in 1978. She retired from Emory University in 2006. She now leads seminars, retreats, and academies across the United States.

For a number of years Bondi was active in Faith and Order both in the National and World Council of Churches. She is committed to the renewal of the church's spiritual life. Her teaching and writing now are in the areas of the early church, spirituality, and narrative. Among her books are *To Love as God Loves: Conversations with the Early Church*; *Memories of God: Theological Reflections on a Life*; *A Place to Pray: Reflections on the Lord's Prayer*; and *Night on the Flint River*.

Recommended by

The Academy
for spiritual Formation®
THE UPPER ROOM

for those who hunger for deep spiritual experience . . .

The Academy for Spiritual Formation® is an experience of disciplined Christian community emphasizing holistic spirituality—nurturing body, mind, and spirit. The program, a ministry of The Upper Room®, is ecumenical in nature and meant for all those who hunger for a deeper relationship with God, including both lay and clergy. Each Academy fosters spiritual rhythms—of study and prayer, silence and liturgy, solitude and relationship, rest and exercise. With offerings of both Two-Year and Five-Day models, Academy participants rediscover Christianity's rich spiritual heritage through worship, learning, and fellowship. The Academy's commitment to an authentic spirituality promotes balance, inner and outer peace, holy living and justice living—God's shalom.

Faculty trained in the wide breadth of Christian spirituality and practice provide content and guidance at each session of The Academy. Academy faculty presenters come from seminaries, monasteries, spiritual direction ministries, and pastoral ministries or other settings and are from a variety of traditions. Author and theologian Roberta Bondi has served as faculty for The Academy for Spiritual Formation for over fifteen years.

The ACADEMY RECOMMENDS program seeks to highlight content that aligns with the Academy's mission to provide resources and settings where pilgrims encounter the teachings, sustaining practices, and rhythms that foster attentiveness to God's Spirit and therefore help spiritual leaders embody Christ's presence in the world.

Learn more here: http://academy.upperroom.org/